ZACHARY TAYLOR
1784-1850

MILLARD FILLMORE
1800-1874

Chronology Documents Bibliographical Aids

Edited by
JOHN J. FARRELL

Series Editor
HOWARD F. BREMER

1971
OCEANA PUBLICATIONS, INC.
Dobbs Ferry, New York 10522

Library of Congress Catalog Card Number: 78-116061

International Standard Book Number: 0-379-12078-X

Manufactured in the United States of America

CONTENTS

BIBLIOGRAPHICAL AIDS

EDITOR'S FOREWORD

Every attempt has been made to cite the most accurate dates in this Chronology. Diaries, documents, letters, and similar evidence have been used to determine the exact date. If, however, later scholarship has found such dates to be obviously erroneous, the more plausible date has been used. Should this Chronology be in conflict with other authorities, the student is urged to go back to original sources as well as to such careful biographers as Arthur Stanley Link.

This is a research tool compiled primarily for the student. While it does make some judgments on the significance of the events, it is hoped that they are reasoned judgments based on a long acquaintance with American History.

Obviously, the very selection of events by any writer is itself a judgment.

The essence of these little books is in their making available some pertinent facts and key documents plus a critical bibliography which should direct the student to investigate for himself additional and/or contradictory material. The works cited may not always be available in small libraries, but neither are they usually the old, out of print, type of book often included in similar accounts.

CHRONOLOGY

YOUTH AND EARLY POLITICS

1784

November 24   Born in Montebello, Orange County, Virginia; the third child of Lieutenant Colonel Richard Taylor and Mary Strother Taylor. Father was a member of one of the oldest families in Virginia and they owned great tracts of land and twenty-six slaves.

1785

April   Moved with family to Jefferson County, Kentucky, very near the present site of Louisville.

Taylor had little formal education, but received some instruction from Kean O'Hara, a noted teacher, on the family plantation.

1808

May 3   Appointed first lieutenant in Kentucky's Seventh Infantry.

1809

April   Placed in command of Fort Pickering (Memphis), Tennessee.

1810

June 21   Married Margaret Mackall Smith, a member of an established Maryland family.

November   Served as Captain of Kentucky's Seventh Infantry, and placed under the command of General William Henry Harrison, governor of the Indiana Territory.

1811

April 9   Daughter, Ann Mackall Taylor, born.

1

1811

November   Gave testimony at the trial of General James Wilkinson, who was accused of conspiring with Aaron Burr to engage in treasonous acts against the United States. Wilkinson was acquitted.

1812

May 3   Took command of Fort Harrison, on the Wabash River, in the Indiana Territory.

June 18   United States declared war on Great Britain.

September 4   Successfully defended Fort Harrison against an attack by Indians; the first United States victory in the War of 1812.

October 31   Appointed brevet major by President James Madison; first brevet commission ever awarded by the United States government.

November 11   Taylor's forces, combined with those of General Samuel Hopkins, destroyed three Indian villages at Prophetstown, near the mouth of the Tippecanoe River.

1813

Recruited, trained, and inspected United States troops in Indiana and Illinois Territories.

September 10   British fleet destroyed by American naval forces on Lake Erie.

1814

March 6   Second daughter, Sarah Knox Taylor, born.

May   Promoted to full rank of line major.

September   Fought military engagements against Indians along the Mississippi River. After removal of the Indian threat in the region, Taylor's rank was reduced to that of captain.

1814

December 24   Treaty of Ghent signed by British and American nego-
               tiators, bringing the War of 1812 to a close.

1815

January 8   General Andrew Jackson led American forces to victory
               against the English invaders at the Battle of New Orleans;
               the battle was fought two weeks after the peace treaty
               was signed.

June   At his own request, Taylor was honorably discharged
               from the Army. He returned to Kentucky to a life of
               farming.

1816

May 17   Restored to rank of major by President James Madison,
               who ordered Taylor to join the Third Infantry at Green
               Bay, Wisconsin.

August 16   Octavia Pennill Taylor, Taylor's third daughter, born
               in Kentucky.

November 25   Arrived at Green Bay, Wisconsin, and commanded forces
               at Fort Winnebago.

1819

April 20   Appointed lieutenant-colonel of the Fourth Infantry; or-
               dered to report to New Orleans.

July 27   Fourth daughter, Margaret Smith Taylor, born in Ken-
               tucky.

August 13   Transferred to Eighth Infantry at his request.

1820

February 20   Arrived in Louisiana, and left soon after to track down
               troublesome Choctaw Indians in the wilderness in and
               around Mississippi.

July 8   Taylor's third daughter, Octavia, died.

1821

August 16   Transferred to Seventh Infantry.

1822

Mrs. Sarah Dabney Strother Taylor, mother of Zachary Taylor, died.

1823

Purchased a cotton plantation in Feliciana Parish, Louisiana, near the border of Mississippi.

Expressed his approval of the principles of the Monroe Doctrine.

1824

April 24   Mary Elizabeth Taylor, Taylor's fifth daughter, born in Kentucky.

Summer   Appointed Superintendent General of Army recruiting service, in the Western Department, with headquarters in Cincinnati, Ohio.

1826

January 27   Richard Taylor, first and only son, born in Kentucky.

October 3   Served on the Board of the Militia, Washington, D.C.

1827

June   Commanded Army troops at Baton Rouge and New Orleans.

1828

May   Took command of Fort Snelling, in the territory of Minnesota.

1829

January 19   Death of Richard Taylor, Taylor's father, in Kentucky.

1829

Spring   In command of Fort Crawford at Prairie du Chien, Mich-
                      igan Territory.

September   Daughter, Ann Taylor, married to Dr. Robert Crooke
                      Wood.

1830

July   Left Fort Crawford, planning to retire.

1831

March 6   Bought 137 acres of land in Wilkinson County, Missis-
                      sippi, adjoining his property in Louisiana.

1832

April-July   Led forces in the Black Hawk War; Jefferson Davis, a
                      graduate of West Point, served as Taylor's adjutant.

August 4   Placed in full command of Fort Crawford. Taylor re-
                      garded the Black Hawk War as a needless waste of men
                      and material.

August 27   Chief Black Hawk captured and placed in Taylor's cus-
                      tody. The famous Indian warrior later mentioned the
                      kind treatment he received from Taylor.

1835

June 17   Sarah Knox Taylor married Jefferson Davis in a wedding
                      ceremony without her parents in attendance. Taylor did
                      not particularly like Davis, but he did not try to influence
                      his daughter in her choice.

September 15   Death of Mrs. Sarah Knox Davis after only three months
                      of marriage. Both Davis and his wife contracted malaria
                      while on their Mississippi plantation. Jefferson Davis
                      spent the following eight years in virtual seclusion.

1836

                      Although never politically involved in any way, Taylor,
                      in his correspondence, noted his dislike of President

1836

Andrew Jackson's policies. In politics, as in religion, Taylor had never aligned himself to any persuasion.

November   In command of Jefferson Barracks, Missouri.

1837

July 31   Received orders to take command of forces in Florida Everglades (Lake Okeechobee). Taylor forced the complete rout of Chief Alligator, who was an ally of Osceola.

1838

May 15   Appointed overall commander of Florida, superseding General Thomas Jesup.

1839

His work proceeded well, and peace reigned throughout the region, until Taylor's policies were undone by Major General Alexander Macomb, General-in-chief of the Army. Macomb's interference left Taylor angered and frustrated. He requested a transfer from Florida.

1840

May 6   Relieved of Florida command at his request, and left to command forces at Baton Rouge. Taylor's Florida command was given to Brigadier General Walker K. Armistead.

1841

April   Transferred from Baton Rouge to command of the Second Department, Western Division, Fort Smith, Arkansas, and Territory west of Arkansas. Taylor sold his Louisiana and Mississippi property before he left for Arkansas with his family.

Taylor was known for his successful diplomatic relations with the various Indian tribes. Peaceful relations continued throughout Taylor's term of command in the southwest, which terminated in 1844. Taylor's aide-

1841
de-camp Captain William S. Bliss, who later became his son-in-law, was known as one of the most skillful and scholarly men in the military.

1842
Paid $95,000 for Cypress Grove Plantation, Jefferson County, Mississippi; eighty-one slaves were included.

1844
April 25 — Ordered to Fort Jesup, Louisiana, and warned to be prepared for action in the event of hostile relations with Mexico over the annexation of Texas.

October — Under Taylor's command at Fort Jesup were three young officers destined to become famous: Second Lieutenant Don Carlos Buell, Second Lieutenant James Longstreet, and Second Lieutenant Ulysses S. Grant.

November 5 — James K. Polk, Tennessee Democrat, elected President of the United States; Polk had advocated the annexation of Texas.

1845
March 1 — President John Tyler, the interregnum executive, approved the annexation of Texas to the United States after successfully promoting approval through a joint Congressional resolution.

June 29 — Received orders from Secretary of Navy George Bancroft to direct his forces to a point near the Rio Grande River.

July 4 — Arrived in New Orleans with eight companies of the Fourth Infantry. On the way, he met his son-in-law Jefferson Davis, a member of Congress from Mississippi, and a firm and lasting friendship developed between the two men.

1845

July 23   Left New Orleans by steamboat for Corpus Christi, Texas, in accordance with the War Department's directive to move "on or near the Rio Grande."

July 26   Landed with three companies of men on St. Joseph's Island, and remained there for four days.

July 31   Arrived in Corpus Christi, Texas, after sailing from St. Joseph's Island. Occupation Army remained in Corpus Christi until the early part of the following year, with total forces numbering almost 4,000.

1846

January 13   Received orders from Secretary of War William Marcy to advance and occupy positions on or near the Rio Grande River. Taylor issued an order to the Mexican communities of Matamoros, Mier, and Corroyo stating that the United States Army would not interfere with the civil or religious rights of any of the inhabitants.

March 24   Encamped with Army on the left bank of the Rio Grande opposite Matamoros and the American flag was raised. Taylor sent a message to General Romolo Diaz de la Vega, Mexico's second in command, that the United States was interested only in safeguarding its own territory.

April 25   A detachment of men sent to investigate an alleged band of Mexican Army men who were spying on United States forces were surrounded by 1600 Mexican soldiers, and sixteen Americans were killed or wounded. Taylor considered the attack a declaration of war, and so informed his superiors in Washington, D.C.

May 1   Led 2,000 men from Fort Texas to Point Isabel, the main supply depot for the American Army.

MEXICAN WAR

May 8   Commanded the Battle of Palo Alto against Mexican army of General Mariano Arista; the opening battle of the Mexican War.

May 9   Battle of Resaca de la Palma; a sweeping victory for Taylor's army over General Arista's defense.

May 13   President James K. Polk signed the Congressionally-approved declaration of the existence of war with Mexico.

June   Thurlow Weed, in his paper, the Albany (New York) Journal, predicted Taylor's election to the presidency. Taylor answered, through his brother Joseph, that he had no political ambitions.

July 18   Received official thanks of the United States Congress for his military achievements.

September 19   Approached city of Monterey with over 6,000 men to eventually meet with more than 7,000 Mexican troops under the command of Major General Pedro de Ampudia.

September 20   General Taylor fought on his feet in the middle of his men, and was admired for his courage and loyalty.

September 25   Monterey fell to the American Army, and a conditional surrender was dictated to the vanquished Mexican army. The victory at Monterey made Taylor a great public hero.

               President Polk and the Democratic Party were not pleased with the popular adulation of Taylor. The President decided to "isolate" Taylor in northern Mexico, and ordered General Winfield S. Scott to command the main American invasion forces to Mexico City.

1847

January 24   Brigham Young led the Mormons into the valley of the
                      Great Salt Lake.

February 23-24   Combined United States forces defeated Santa Anna's
                      army at Buena Vista, a turning point in the Mexican
                      War. Taylor's forces were outnumbered four to one.
                      Although a great victory, Taylor deplored the loss of
                      nearly 700 American men; he placed the blame on
                      President Polk and Secretary of War William Marcy
                      for being politically partisan, and not giving him
                      adequate numbers of regular fighting men.

                      Taylor's forces were not given permission to enter
                      into the final thrusts of the war around Mexico City.
                      Taylor interpreted this as a Presidential effort to keep
                      him out of the public eye as much as possible.

April-October   Held camp at Walnut Springs, near Monterey. During
                      this rather dormant period, he began to develop some
                      political interest. In a letter to his political friend
                      Joseph Ingersoll, Taylor noted he would not be adverse
                      to the Presidency if he were the choice of the people
                      of the country; he had no use for any party affiliation.
                      His natural congeniality made him very popular with
                      the press and he became one of the most admired men
                      in America.

July   Georgia's Whig Party met in convention and endorsed
                      Taylor for the Presidency; Alexander Stephens, a po-
                      litical power in the South, instigated the move to Taylor.

September 4   Nominated for Presidency by the Native American
                      Party in convention at Philadelphia.

September 13   Chapultepec Hill was taken by United States forces.

September 14   Mexico City fell and the United States flag was flown
                      over the Mexican National Palace.

1847

November 26   Left Mexican territory and boarded ship for New Orleans.

December 3   Received the tribute of the people of New Orleans in special ceremonies in his honor.

December 5   Left New Orleans for Baton Rouge, where another reception awaited him. Settled in his home, called the "Spanish Cottage," near the city of Baton Rouge. He remained there for thirteen months.

1848

January 1   A Zachary Taylor-Daniel Webster Presidential ticket was proposed by the New York Courier and Empire.

January   In a joint resolution, the Tennessee legislature recommended the selection of Taylor as the candidate of the Whig Party.

January 20   Suffered an attack of rheumatism; invalided for almost five weeks.

January 24   Gold discovered on the property of John Sutter, near Sacramento, California, thus precipitating the "Gold Rush" of 1849.

February 2   Treaty of Guadalupe-Hidalgo signed by Mexico and the United States. The treaty provided that the Rio Grande River would serve as the southern boundary of Texas, and the territories of New Mexico and Upper California would be ceded to the United States. Mexico was paid $15 million for her lost provinces.

THE GENERAL IN POLITICS

February-   In letters to friends, his opposition to Polk's adminis-
April   tration was given vent and he again expressed himself as a possible President, only with the support

1848

of the "people" of the country. His natural aversion to the Democratic Party, he noted, probably made him a Whig.

Never having held political office, Taylor had to be "sold" to the public by Whig functionaries. Thurlow Weed, the New York Whig Party boss and editor of the influential Albany Evening Journal, began to play a major role in "educating" the public. Other supporters were former governor William H. Seward of New York, Alexander H. Stephens and Robert Toombs, both members of the Georgia House of Representatives, and Senators John J. Crittenden and John M. Clayton of Kentucky.

April 10

Henry Clay of Kentucky announced his candidacy for the Whig nomination for the Presidency. Clay had already been defeated three times for the presidential office. Whig Party forces were disinclined to press for Clay's candidacy, and privately manoeuvered strength to Taylor.

By the end of April, only Taylor and General Winfield S. Scott were considered acceptable bidders for the presidential nomination by most Whigs.

April 20

Taylor, in a letter to the press, stated he would not refuse a Whig nomination.

April 21

In a letter to his brother-in-law, John Stadler Allison, Taylor declared himself a Whig, but said he would not consent to be a party-controlled President.

May 22-26

Democratic National Convention met in Baltimore. President Polk had announced his firm decision not to run again for office. General Lewis Cass of Michigan was nominated for President, and General William O. Butler of Kentucky for Vice-President. The Democrats

1848

deliberately fashioned a platform that took no position on the question of slavery in the newly acquired lands in the West.

June 6   A caucus was held by the Whig leaders in New York City at which pro-Taylor supporters pleaded with Henry Clay and Daniel Webster adherents to give their support to Taylor.

June 7-9   About 300 delegates of the Whig Party met in Philadelphia to choose a Presidential candidate. Neither Henry Clay nor Daniel Webster had given up hope for the nomination, and had instructed their delegates to hold fast to their votes.

A majority of 140 votes were needed to win, and Taylor led on the first ballot with an agreeable 111 votes. Clay was second with 97 votes, General Winfield Scott, third with 43 votes, and Daniel Webster trailed behind with 22 votes.

On the second ballot, Taylor moved forward to a total of 118 votes; Clay's strength decreased to 86 votes, and General Scott's to 49.

The third round found Connecticut and Maryland's ballots deserting Clay, and Taylor's count advanced to 133, with only seven needed to win. Clay's count had suffered a decline to 74, and Scott held 54.

Taylor won the nomination on the fourth ballot, when Webster's delegates gave their votes to Taylor. The final count read: Taylor, 171; Scott, 63; Clay, 32; Webster, 14.

New Englanders were especially angry with the selection of Taylor, a southern slave-owner, and Charles Francis Adams of Massachusetts went so far as to suggest that the Whig Party simply cease to exist.

1848

Fourteen men were nominated for the Vice-Presidency, including Thurlow Weed of New York. Abbott Lawrence of New York, a millionaire and generous party contributor, was a favored candidate, as was Thomas Ewing of Ohio, and Millard Fillmore of New York. Fillmore was an experienced politician and a founder of the Whig Party. Fillmore won the nomination over Lawrence on the second ballot.

No platform was adopted since whatever might be said about important national problems would alienate at least one or more sections of the country.

June 14-15   The National Liberty Party nominated Gerrit Smith of New York as the Presidential candidate, and Charles Foote of Michigan as the Vice-Presidential candidate.

June 22   A splinter group of the Democratic Party, called the Barnburners, met in convention in Utica, New York, to nominate a candidate dedicated to the nonextension of slavery into the new territories. Ex-President Martin Van Buren was chosen by acclamation, and Senator Henry Dodge of Wisconsin was selected as his running mate.

June 28   A group of 7,000 radical Whigs met in Worcester, Massachusetts, under the leadership of Senator Charles Sumner and Charles Francis Adams. Joshua Gidding, a renowned anti-slave orator, prevailed on the delegates to support Martin Van Buren for the Presidency at the Free Soil Convention.

July-
October   Taylor's Presidential campaign ran almost entirely on his "Rough and Ready" image, and the fact that he was a man of "the people."

August 9   Free Soil Party met in Buffalo, New York. Martin Van Buren was chosen the Presidential candidate, and

1848

Charles Francis Adams of Massachusetts the Vice-
Presidential candidate. Their platform was summed
up in the cry: "Free soil, free speech, free labor,
and free men!"

September 4   With the assistance of Alexander C. Bullitt, the editor
of the New Orleans Picayune, Taylor attempted to
clarify some contradictory statements and to present
himself as a firm believer for the cause of Union.

October   Several states elected Whig governors, including Pennsylvania and Ohio. Abraham Lincoln, a Whig congressman from Illinois, denounced the Free Soil Party candidate and endorsed Taylor.

November 7   Elected 12th President of the United States. Taylor
carried 15 states, as did Lewis Cass, the Democratic
candidate, but Taylor took the heavily weighted electoral states of New York, Massachusetts, and Pennsylvania. The popular vote was 1,360,000 for Taylor,
1,220,000 for Cass, 291,263 for Van Buren, and 2,733
for Gerrit Smith.

The electoral vote, out of a possible 290: Taylor, 163;
Cass, 127, none for Van Buren or Smith.

December 5   Gave his daughter Mary Elizabeth (Betsy) Taylor in
marriage to William Wallace Smith Bliss. Bliss was
known as a brilliant military man and an accomplished
linguist.

1849

January 13   Virginia Resolves were passed by that State's legislature declaring that it would oppose any federal legislation interfering with southern institutions, and would
seek redress if such action occurred.

1849

January 22   Caucus of slave state members of Congress called to listen to Senator John C. Calhoun's Southern Address and to take action to forestall any Northern aggression against the South.

January 23   Taylor retired from the United States Army, in which he had served for 40 years.

February 23   Arrived in Washington, D. C.

February 25   Made a social call to the White House to greet President Polk.

March 3   The Territory of Minnesota was established, and slavery was forbidden.

March 4   Congress created the Department of the Interior to relieve the Treasury Department of coping with the problems of public lands and Indian affairs.

THE PRESIDENCY

March 5   Zachary Taylor was sworn in as 12th President of the United States. March 4th, the day set aside for the Inauguration, fell on a Sunday, thus the oath of office was administered the following day. Some historical buffs have suggested that the President pro tem of the Senate, David Rice Atchinson of Missouri, was President for one day, since President Polk's term had ended at noon on March 4th, and Vice President George M. Dallas had resigned on March 2nd.

Taylor's Inaugural Address placed emphasis on executive "conciliation" with Congress, an arrangement which would "tend to perpetrate the Union." Taylor offered no solution to the question of slavery expansion. (See Documents.)

1849

March   Taylor's cabinet appointments included: John Mid-
               dleton Clayton of Delaware, Secretary of State; Wil-
               liam Morris Meredith of Pennsylvania, Secretary of
               Treasury; George Washington Crawford of Georgia,
               Secretary of War; Reverdy Johnson of Maryland, At-
               torney General; Jacob Collamer of Vermont, Post-
               master General; William Bellard Preston of Virginia,
               Secretary of Navy; and Thomas Ewing of Ohio, ap-
               pointed the nation's first Secretary of the Interior.

               The Democratic Party noted the power of the new cab-
               inet and intimated a "controlled" executive.

June 3   A "civil government" in California was announced by
               its initiator General Bennett Riley, commander of
               American forces. Taylor was presented with the task
               of deciding on the status of the new region.

June 4   Thomas Butler King, of Georgia, acting as Taylor's
               special agent, arrived in San Francisco. King ex-
               pressed the President's desire to see California enter
               as a state and not a territory.

June 13   Ex-President James K. Polk died in Nashville, Ten-
               nessee, just three months after his retirement.

November 13   People of California accepted a proposed state con-
               stitution prohibiting slavery.

December 4   In his annual message, Taylor recommended state-
               hood for California and asked the nation and Congress
               to avoid the issue of slavery.

December 20   Newly adopted constitution of California went into ef-
               fect, and plans were made for its early admission
               to the Union as a free state. Statehood for California,
               however, would mean the end of the balance between
               free and slave states.

1849

Taylor's southern colleagues resisted the entrance of California as a free state, and some southern congressmen considered Taylor a traitor to the southern Whigs.

December   The animosity that existed between North and South, Democrat and Whig was especially noted at the opening session of the 31st Congress, when the House was unable to agree on the selection of the Speaker. After sixty-three ballots and three weeks, Howell Cobb of Georgia was finally selected.

December 27-28   Resolutions introduced in both Houses of Congress illustrated the North-South impasse over the question of slavery in the new territories; the North promoted the Wilmot Proviso principle; the South found any restrictions on slave expansion intolerable.

1850

January 16   Senator Thomas Hart Benton of Missouri, on the Senate floor, demanded that Texas surrender any of her claims to New Mexican territory, and suggested that Texas be paid $15 million for this concession.

January 21   In a special message to Congress, Taylor pleaded for California's early admission to the Union, and suggested New Mexico be entered on the basis of popular sovereignty at a later date.

Congressman Thomas L. Clingham of North Carolina proclaimed the right of secession in the event of any federal legislation prohibiting slavery expansion.

January 29   Henry Clay of Kentucky proposed eight resolutions to end the national stalemate on the western lands:

1. California would be admitted as a free state.
2. Territorial governments would be created for New Mexican lands, with no decision on slavery.

1850

3. Texas' western boundary would be fixed to exclude all of New Mexico.
4. The United States would assume the public debt of Texas.
5. Slave trade would be prohibited in Washington, D.C.
6. Slavery would continue to exist in Washington, D.C., unless slave owners agreed to its abolition.
7. A more effective Fugitive Slave Act should be passed for the "restitution and delivery" of runaway slaves.
8. Congress would state that it had no right to interfere with slave trade.

Clay proposed that all eight resolutions be passed as a package without having to resort to interminable debate on each.

February 5-6 President Taylor refused to support Clay's compromise proposals, and was chagrined that neither Clay nor Senator Daniel Webster had even consulted with him.

February 13 Sent California's constitution to Congress for a vote, but southern representatives refused to consider California without other provisions that would call for some northern compromise.

February 19 Leading northern and southern congressmen agreed to accept a compromise solution on the California question.

February Sir Henry Lytton-Bulwer of Great Britain and Secretary of State John Clayton drafted numerous proposals on the question of joint United States-Great Britain jurisdiction over a canal through Central America. The negotiators agreed that each country would insure complete neutrality over the waterway, and each would attempt to secure capital investments for its construction.

1850

President Taylor was unwilling to approve the draft of the treaty without Great Britain's agreement to relinquish her control over certain Nicaraguan territory, called (by England) the Mosquito protectorate.

After weeks of argument, Lord Palmerston agreed to clauses in a proposed canal treaty stating (because of President Taylor's insistence) that there would be no " . . . dominion over . . . the Mosquito coast, or any part of Central America."

March 7

For three hours Senator Daniel Webster of Massachusetts eloquently pleaded with the Senate to accept Henry Clay's proposals. Webster's only concern was, he said, the preservation of the Union, and roundly condemned the extremists of both North and South. Over 12,000 copies of the speech were circulated, and the American people enthusiastically made known their support.

March 11

Appealing to "a higher law" than the Constitution of the United States, New York's Senator William Seward stated his anti-slave position in a speech to the Senate. Seward's declamation came as a blow to the President since Seward was a trusted adviser and the President strongly condemned the attack on slavery.

March 13

Senator Stephen A. Douglas of Illinois proclaimed his belief in popular sovereignty as a means of solving the New Mexican land stalemate. He attacked the general belief that territories belonged to North or South, and stated that they belong to all the people. Douglas, therefore, threw his support to Senator Clay's proposals.

President Taylor continued to support his own belief that California should be admitted as a free state, and that all other matters should be treated separately.

1850

March 31   Death of Senator John C. Calhoun was announced. The
                  "voice of the South" had fought for the cause of south-
                  ern rights until the moment of death.

April 2   President Taylor and his cabinet attended Senator John
                  C. Calhoun's funeral at the nation's capital. Senator
                  Henry Clay gave the eulogy and stressed his affection
                  for his former colleague.

April 17   **Senators Thomas H.** Benton of Missouri and Henry
                  Foote of Mississippi symbolized the intensity of the
                  growing sectional gap by referring to each other as
                  "treasonous" and "assassin."

                  Senator Henry S. Foote proposed to the Senate that a
                  committee of thirteen be established to consider solu-
                  tions to the continued stalemate; the Senate agreed
                  30-22 in favor of such a committee. Senator Henry
                  Clay served as Chairman of the Select Committee, and
                  a series of seven proposals (similar to Clay's original
                  recommendations) were later reported to the Senate.

                  President Taylor continued to oppose any acceptance
                  of a solution that would tie the statehood of California
                  to a settlement of the lands of New Mexico and Utah.

April 19   Secretary of State John M. Clayton and Britain's Sir
                  Henry Lytton-Bulwer signed the proposed treaty a-
                  greement for a canal through Central America.

April 22   Delivered the proposed canal agreement to the Senate
                  for ratification, which was done by both Democrats
                  and Whigs in a rare show of agreement.

April-June   The Senate and the House of Representatives continued
                  the "Great Debate." Eventually, the emotional nature
                  of the North-South argument began to show signs of
                  weakening for a more moderate point of view.

1850

May   Attempt to "free" Cuba from Spain was led by the
               anti-Spanish Cuban General Narcisco Lopez. The ex-
               pedition was launched from Louisiana.

               Lopez and a band of Americans aboard the Creole
               seized the city of Cardenes, eighty miles east of Ha-
               vana. The group was soon in retreat; over seventy
               American men were killed in the debacle.

               President Taylor demanded prosecution of the adven-
               turers, but the sympathies of the Louisiana people lay
               with Lopez, and the subsequent trial was judged a
               farce. Louisiana acquitted the entire group, and the
               final outcome of the trial further increased the strained
               feelings between Spain and the United States.

May 20   President Taylor was strongly criticized by Senator
               Henry Clay in remarks made on the Senate floor.
               Clay's attack was based on what he believed to be a
               dangerous course against compromise taken by the
               President.

May 27   In the Whig newspaper, The Republic, President Taylor
               criticized Senator Henry Clay for not being truthful
               about the Presidential plan for settling the land stale-
               mate.

May 28   Ex-President John Tyler, in a letter to the Washington
               Union, supported Senator Clay's compromise pro-
               posals, and urged President Taylor to accept the com-
               promise.

June 4   Representatives of nine slaveholding states (Delaware,
               Kentucky, Louisiana, Maryland, Missouri, and North
               Carolina were not represented) met in Nashville, Ten-
               nessee. The delegates resolved that the nation should
               be warned that the South would countenance no inter-
               ference with slavery, and that the Missouri Compro-
               mise line be extended to the Pacific Ocean. Their

1850

ultimate solution to northern autocracy was secession from the Union.

June 17   In a special message to Congress, Taylor informed the representatives that Texas was attempting to define its boundaries to include parts of New Mexico within her jurisdiction. He asked Congress to protect the interests of New Mexico. New Mexico, in the meantime, had designed a possible territorial constitution prohibiting slavery.

July 1   When Texas threatened imminent action against New Mexico in order to claim her alleged territory, Taylor declared that he would use all the forces at his command to check Texas action. If his death had not occurred shortly after, he might have sent troops against Texas.

July 3   Taylor met with Georgia Whig spokesmen Senator Robert Toombs and Representative Alexander H. Stephens. They told Taylor that the South would not forgive the President if Texas was not allowed her own boundaries as she saw them (including New Mexico). The President considered any Whig deviation from his set position disloyalty to the Party.

July 4   Attended various Independence Day ceremonies and later in the day became ill with acute gastroenteritis, which advanced into high fever.

July 5   As his last official act, Taylor signed the Clayton-Bulwer Treaty from his bed.

July 7   Announced from his bed that he would die in two days.

July 9   Died at 10:35 p.m.

1850

July 13   A two-mile funeral procession advanced to the Con-
                     gressional Cemetery. Taylor's famous horse "Old
                     Whitey" followed the cortege with empty saddle and
                     reversed boots in the stirrups. Senators Henry Clay
                     and Daniel Webster were among the pallbearers.

July 18   Mrs. Taylor left Washington, D.C., to live with her
                     daughter Betsy and Betsy's husband William Bliss, in
                     New Orleans. She died two years later.

October 25   Taylor's remains were removed from Washington,
                     D.C., to Pittsburgh, Pennsylvania, then by river to
                     Springfield, Kentucky, his original home.

INAUGURAL ADDRESS*
March 5, 1849

After a campaign entirely devoid of specific statements pertaining to the most important problems facing the nation, the new President's inaugural address followed similarly. One of the shortest inaugural addresses on record, it basically outlined the nature of the Chief Executive's role in the federal structure, interpreted, of course, by President Taylor. That the White House would contain no maverick is indicated by the President's remarks about looking "...with confidence to the enlightened patriotism of that body...", i.e., the Congress, for direction of Presidential policy. Even Taylor's fellow Whigs were reluctant to prejudge the new President's activities in the light of his vacuous address.

Elected by the American people to the highest office known to our laws, I appear here to take the oath presecribed by the Constitution, and, in compliance with a time-honored custom, ta address those who are now assembled.

The confidence and respect shown by my countrymen in calling me to be the Chief Magistrate of a Republic holding a high rank among the nations of the earth have inspired me with feelings of the most profound gratitude; but when I reflect that the acceptance of the office which their partiality has bestowed imposes the discharge of the most arduous duties and involves the weightiest obligations, I am conscious that the position which I have been called to fill, though sufficient to satisfy the loftiest ambition, is surrounded by fearful responsibilities. Happily, however, in the performance of my new duties I shall not be without able cooperation. The legislative and judicial branches of the Government present prominent examples of distinguished civil attainments and matured experience, and it shall by me endeavor to call to my assistance in the Executive Departments individuals whose talents, integrity, and purity of character will furnish ample guaranties for the faithful and honorable performance of the trusts to be committed to their charge. With such aids and an honest purpose to do whatever is right, I hope to execute diligently, impartially, and for the best interests of the country the manifold duties devolved upon me.

---

*James Richardson, ed. *Messages and Papers of the Presidents*, Vol. 6, New York, 1897, pp. 2551–2556.

In the discharge of these duties my guide will be the Constitution, which I this day swear to "preserve, protect, and defend." For the interpretation of that instrument I shall look to the decisions of the judicial tribunals established by its authority and to the practice of the Government under the earlier Presidents, who had so large a share in its formation. To the example of those illustrious patriots I shall always defer with reverence, and especially to his example who was by so many titles "the Father of his Country."

To command the Army and Navy of the United States; with the advice and consent of the Senate, to make treaties and to appoint ambassadors and other officers; to give to Congress information of the state of the Union and recommend such measures as he shall judge to be necessary; and to take care that the laws shall be faithfully executed — these are the most important functions intrusted to the President by the Constitution, and it may be expected that I shall briefly indicate the principles which will control me in their execution.

Chosen by the body of the people under the assurance that my Administration would be devoted to the welfare of the whole country, and not to the support of any particular section or merely local interest, I this day renw the declarations I have heretofore made and proclaim my fixed determination to maintain to the extent of my ability the Government in its original purity and to adopt as the basis of my public policy those great republican doctrines which constitute the strength of our national existence.

In reference to the Army and Navy, lately employed with so much distinction on active service, care shall be taken to insure the highest condition of efficiency, and in furtherance of that object the military and naval schools, sustained by the liberality of Congress, shall receive the special attention of the Executive.

As American freemen we can not but sympathize in all efforts to extend the blessings of civil and political liberty, but at the same time we are warned by the admonitions of history and the voice of our own beloved Washington to abstain from entangling alliances with foreign nations. In all disputes between conflicting governments it is our interest not less than our duty to remain strictly neutral, while our geographical position, the genius of our institutions and our people, the advancing spirit of civilization, and, above all, the dictates of religion direct us to the cultivation of peaceful and friendly relations with all other powers. It is to be hoped that no international question can now arise which a government confident in its own strength and resolved to protect its own just rights may not settle by wise negotiation; and it eminently becomes a government like our own, founded on the morality and intelligence of its citizens and upheld by their affections, to exhaust every resort of honorable diplomacy before appealing to arms. In the conduct of our foreign relations I shall conform to these views, as I believe them essential to the best interests and the honor of the country.

The appointing power vested in the President imposes delicate and onerous duties. So far as it is possible to be informed, I shall make honesty, capacity, and fidelity indispensable prerequisites to the bestowal of office, and the absence of either of these qualities shall be deemed sufficient cause for removal.

It shall be my study to recommend such constitutional measures to Congress as may be necessary and proper to secure encouragement and protection to the great interests of agriculture, commerce, and manufactures, to improve our rivers and harbors, to provide for the speedy extinguishment of the public debt, to enforce a strict accountability on the part of all officers of the Government and the utmost economy in all public expenditures; but it is for the wisdom of Congress itself, in which all legislative powers are vested by the Constitution, to regulate these and other matters of domestic policy. I shall look with confidence to the enlightened patriotism of that body to adopt such measures of conciliation as may harmonize conflicting interests and tend to perpetuate that Union which should be the paramount object of our hopes and affections. In any action calculated to promote an object so near the heart of everyone who truly loves his country I will zealously unite with the coordinate branches of the Government.

In conclusion I congratulate you, my fellow-citizens, upon the high state of prosperity to which the goodness of Divine Providence has conducted our common country. Let us invoke a continuance of the same protecting care which has led us from small beginnings to the eminence we this day occupy, and let us seek to deserve that continuance prudence and moderation in our councils, by well-directed attempts to assuage the bitterness which too often marks unavoidable differences of opinion, by the promulgation and practice of just and liberal principles, and by an enlarged patriotism, which shall acknowledge no limits but those of our own wide-spread Republic.

FIRST ANNUAL MESSAGE*
December 4, 1849

The following excerpts from President Taylor's first and only annual address to Congress depict the growing complexity of the nation. A departure from traditional disinterest with foreign affairs is noteworthy; the warning against forays to Cuba; sympathy, but not support, to Kossuth's revolutionary group in Hungary; expressed interest in formulating a desirable treaty with Great Britain for a canal in Central America — all are mentioned in the address.

Growing tension between Congress and the President was provoked by Taylor in the passage calling for California's statehood, rather than territorial status. His clear statement lay the foundation for the dispute that was to culminate only after the death of Taylor in the Compromise of 1850.

The last section of the address reflects Taylor's belief in the presidential office as one that enjoys a certain independence of action, but one that reacts to the decision powers of Congress. Taylor was most anxious to set an agreeable stage for the coming sectional storm concerning the new lands of the west.

. . . Having been apprised that a considerable number of adventurers were engaged in fitting out a military expedition within the United States against a foreign country, and believing from the best information I could obtain that it was destined to invade the island of Cuba, I deemed it due to the friendly relations existing between the United States and Spain, to the treaty between the two nations, to the laws of the United States, and, above all, to the American honor to exert the lawful authority of this Government in suppressing the expedition and preventing the invasion. To this end I issued a proclamation enjoining it upon the officers of the United States, civil and military, to use all lawful means within their power. A copy of that proclamation is herewith submitted. The expedition has been suppressed. So long as the act of Congress of the 20th of April, 1818, which owes its existence to the law of nations and to the policy of Washington himself, shall remain in our statute books, I hold it to be the duty of the Executive faithfully to obey its injunctions.

While this expedition was in progress I was informed that a foreigner who claimed our protection had been clandestinely and, as was sup-

---

*James Richardson, ed. *Messages and Papers of the Presidents*, Vol. 6, New York, 1897. pp. 2558–2563.

posed, forcibly carried off in a vessel from New Orleans to the island of Cuba. I immediately caused such steps to be taken as I thought necessary, in case the information I had received should prove correct, to vindicate the honor of the country and the right of every person seeking an asylum on our soil to the protection of our laws. The person alleged to have been abducted was promptly restored, and the circumstances of the case are now about to undergo investigation before a judicial tribunal. I would respectfully suggest that although the crime charged to have been committed in this case is held odious, as being in conflict with our opinions on the subject of national sovereignty and personal freedom, there is no prohibition of it or punishment for it provided in any act of Congress. The expedience of supplying this defect in our criminal code is therefore recommended to your consideration.

I have scrupulously avoided any interference in the wars and contentions which have recently distracted Europe. During the late conflict between Austria and Hungary there seemed to be a prospect that the latter might become an independent nation. However faint that prospect at the time appeared, I thought it my duty, in accordance with the general sentiment of the American people, who deeply sympathized with the Magyars. The United States did not at any time interfere in the contest, but the feelings of the nation were strongly enlisted in the cause, and by the sufferings of a brave people, who had made a gallant, though unsuccessful effort to be free. . . .

With Russia, Austria, Prussia, Sweden, Denmark, Belgium, the Netherlands, and the Italian States we still maintain our accustomed amicable relations.

During the recent revolutions in the Papal States our charge d'affaires at Rome has been unable to present his letter of credence, which, indeed, he was directed by my predecessor to withhold until he should receive further orders. Such was the unsettled condition of things in those States that it was not deemed expedient to give him any instructions on the subject of presenting his credential letter different from those with which he had been furnished by the late Administration until the 25th of June last, when, in consequence of the want of accurate information of the exact state of things at that distance from us, he was instructed to exercise his own discretion in presenting himself to the then existing Government if in his judgment sufficiently stable, or, if not, to await further events. Since that period Rome has undergone another revolution, and he abides the establishment of a government sufficiently permanent to justify him in opening diplomatic intercourse with it.

With the Republic of Mexico it is our true policy to cultivate the most friendly relations. Since the ratification of the treaty of Guadalupe Hidalgo nothing has occurred of a serious character to disturb them. A faithful observance of the treaty and a sincere respect for her rights cannot fail to secure the lasting confidence and friendship of that Republic. The message of my predecessor to the House of Representatives of the 8th of February last, communicating, in compliance with a resolution of that body, a copy of a paper called a protocol, signed at Queretaro on the 30th of May, 1848, by the commissioners of the United States and the minister of foreign affairs of the Mexican Government, having been a subject of correspondence between the Department of State and the envoy extraordinary and minister plenipotentiary of that Republic accredited to this Government, a transcript of that correspondence is herewith submitted. . . .

In the adjustment of the claims of American citizens on Mexico, provided for by the late treaty, the employment of counsel on the part of the Government may become important for the purpose of assisting the commissioners in protecting the interests of the United States. I recommend this subject to the early and favorable consideration of Congress.

Complaints have been made in regard to the inefficiency of the means provided by the Government of New Granada for transporting the United States mail across the Isthmus of Panama, pursuant to our postal convention with that Republic of the 6th of March, 1844. Our charge d'affaires at Bogota has been directed to make such representations to the Government of New Granada as will, it is hoped, lead to a prompt removal of this cause of complaint.

The sanguinary civil war with which the Republic of Venezuela has for some time past been ravaged has been brought to a close. In its progress the rights of some of our citizens resident or trading there have been violated. The restoration of order will afford the Venezuelan Government an opportunity to examine and redress these grievances and others of longer standing which our representatives at Caracas have hitherto ineffectually urged upon the attention of that Government.

The extension of the coast of the United States on the Pacific and the unexampled rapidity with which the inhabitants of California especially are increasing in numbers have imparted new consequence to our relations with the other countries whose territories border upon that ocean. It is probably that the intercourse between those countries and our possessions in that quarter, particularly with the Republic of Chili, will become extensive and mutually advantageous in proportion as California and Oregon shall increase in population and wealth. It is desirable, therefore, that this Government should do everything in its power to foster and strengthen its relations with those States, and that the spirit of amity between us should be mutual and cordial.

I recommend the observance of the same course toward all other American States. The United States stand as the great American power, to which, as their natural ally and friend, they will always be disposed first to look for mediation and assistance in the event of any collision between them and any European nation. As such we may often kindly mediate in their behalf without entangling ourselves in foreign wars or unnecessary controversies. Whenever the faith of our treaties with any of them shall require our interference, we must necessarily interpose.

A convention has been negotiated with Brazil providing for the satisfaction of American claims on that Government, and it will be submitted to the Senate. Since the last session of Congress we have received an envoy extraordinary and minister plenipotentiary from that Empire, and our relations with it are founded upon the most amicable understanding.

Your attention is earnestly invited to an amendment of our existing laws relating to the African slave trade with a view to the effectual suppression of that barbarous traffic. It is not to be denied that this trade is still in part carried on by means of vessels built in the United States and owned or navigated by some of our citizens. The correspondence between the Department of State and the minister and consul of the United States at Rio de Janeiro, which has from time to time been laid before Congress, represents that it is a customary device to evade the penalties of our laws by means of sea letters. Vessels sold in Brazil, when provided with such papers by the consul, instead of returning to the United States for a new register proceed at once to the coast of Africa for the purpose of obtaining cargoes of slaves. Much additional information of the same character has recently been transmitted to the Department of State. It has not been considered the policy of our laws to subject an American citizen who in a foreign country purchases a vessel built in the United States to the inconvenience of sending her home for a new register before permitting her to proceed on a voyage. Any alteration of the laws which might have a tendency to impede the free transfer of property in vessels between our citizens, or the free navigation of those vessels between different parts of the world when employed in lawful commerce, should be well and cautiously considered; but I trust that your wisdom will devise a method by which our general policy in this respect may be preserved, and at the same time the abuse of our flag by means of sea letters, in the manner indicated, may be prevented.

Having ascertained that there is no prospect of the reunion of the five States of Central America which formerly composed the Republic of that name, we have separately negotiated with some of them treaties of amity and commerce, which will be laid before the Senate.

A contract having been concluded with the State of Nicaragua by a company composed of American citizens for the purpose of constructing a ship canal through the territory of that State to connect the Atlantic and Pacific oceans, I have directed the negotiation of a treaty with Nicaragua pledging both Governments to protect those who shall engage in and perfect the work. All other nations are invited by the State of Nicaragua to enter into the same treaty stipulations with her; and the benefit to be derived by each from such an arrangement will be the protection of this great interoceanic communication against any power which might seek to obstruct it or to monopolize its advantages. All States entering into such a treaty will enjoy the right of passage through the canal on payment of the same tolls. The work, if constructed under these guaranties, will become a bond of peace instead of a subject of contention and strife between the nations of the earth. Should the great maritime States of Europe consent to this arrangement (and we have no reason to suppose that a proposition so fair and honorable will be opposed by any), the energies of their people and ours will cooperate in promoting the success of the enterprise. I do not recommend any appropriation from the National Treasury for this purpose, nor do I believe that such an appropriation is necessary. Private enterprise, if properly protected, will complete the work should it prove to be feasible. The parties who have procured the charter from Nicaragua for its construction desire no assistance from this Government beyond its protection; and they profess that, having examined the proposed line of communication, they will be ready to commence the undertaking whenever that protection shall be extended to them. Should there appear to be reason, on examining the whole evidence, to entertain a serious doubt of the practicability of constructing such a canal, that doubt could be speedily solved by an actual exploration of the route.

Should such a work be constructed under the common protection of all nations, for equal benefits to all, it would be neither just nor expedient that any great maritime state should command the communication. The territory through which the canal may be opened ought to be freed from the claims of any foreign power. No such power should occupy a position that would enable it hereafter to exercise so controlling an influence over the commerce of the world or to obstruct a highway which ought to be dedicated to the common uses of mankind.

The routes across the Isthmus at Tehuantepec and Panama are also worthy of our serious consideration. They did not fail to engage the attention of my predecessor. The negotiator of the treaty of Guadalupe Hidalgo was instructed to offer a very large sum of money for the right of transit across the Isthmus of Tehuantepec. The Mexican Government did not accede to the proposition for the purchase of the right of way, probably because it had already contracted with private individuals for the construction of a passage from the Guasacualco River to Tehuantepec. I shall not renew any proposition to purchase for money a right which ought to be equally secured to all nations on payment of a reasonable toll to the owners of the improvement, who would doubtless be well contented with that compensation and the guaranties of the maritime states of the world in separate treaties negotiated with Mexico, binding her and them to protect those who should construct the work. Such guaranties would do more to secure the completion of the communication through the territory of Mexico than any other reasonable consideration that could be offered; and as Mexico herself would be the greatest gainer by the opening of this communication between the Gulf and the Pacific Ocean, it is presumed that she would not hesitate to yield her aid in the manner proposed to accomplish an improvement so important to her own best interests.

We have reason to hope that the proposed railroad across the Isthmus at Panama will be successfully constructed under the protection of the late treaty with New Granada, ratified and exchanged by my predecessor on the 10th day of June, 1848, which guarantees the perfect neutrality of the Isthmus and the rights of sovereignty and property of New Granada over that territory, "with a view that the free transit from ocean to ocean may not be interrupted or embarrassed" during the existence of the treaty. It is our policy to encourage every practicable route across the isthmus which connects North and South America, either by railroad or canal, which the energy and enterprise of our citizens may induce them to complete, and I consider it obligatory upon me to adopt that policy, especially in consequence of the absolute necessity of facilitating intercourse with our possessions on the Pacific. . . .

I recommend a revision of the existing tariff and its adjustment on a basis which may augment the revenue. I do not doubt the right or duty of Congress to encourage domestic industry, which is the great source of national as well as individual wealth and prosperity. I look to the wisdom and patriotism of Congress for the adoption of a system which may place home labor at last on a sure and permanent footing and by due encouragement of manufactures give a new and increased stimulus to agriculture and promote the development of our vast resources and the extension of our commerce. Believing that to the attainment of these ends, as well as the necessary augmentation of the revenue and the prevention of frauds, a system of specific duties is best adapted, I strongly recommend to Congress the adoption of that system, fixing the duties at rates high enough to afford substantial and sufficient encouragement to our own industry and at the same time so adjusted as to insure stability. . . .

No civil government having been provided by Congress for California, the people of that Territory, impelled by the necessities of their political condition, recently met in convention for the purpose of forming a constitution and State government, which the latest advices give me reason to suppose has been accomplished; and it is believed they will shortly apply for the admission of California into the Union as a sovereign State. Should such be the case, and should their constitution be conformable to the requisitions of the Constitution of the United States, I recommend their application to the favorable consideration of Congress. The people of New Mexico will also, it is believed, at no very distant period present themselves for admission into the Union. Preparatory to the admission of California and New Mexico the people of each will have instituted for themselves a republican form of government, "laying its foundation in such principles and organizing its powers in such form as to them shall seem most likely to effect their safety and happiness." By awaiting their action all causes of uneasiness may be avoided and confidence and kind feeling preserved. With a view of maintaining the harmony and tranquility so dear to all, we should abstain from the introduction of those exciting topics of a sectional character which hitherto produced painful apprehensions in the public mind; and I repeat the solemn warning of the first and most illustrious of my predecessors against furnishing "any ground for characterizing parties by geographical discriminations.". . .

The great mineral wealth of California and the advantages which its ports and harbors and those of Oregon afford to commerce, especially with the islands of the Pacific and Indian oceans and the populous regions of eastern Asia, make it certain that there will arise in a few years large and prosperous communities on our western coast. It therefore becomes important that a line of communication, the best and most expeditious which the nature of the country will admit, should be opened within the territory of the United States from the navigable waters of the Atlantic or the Gulf of Mexico to the Pacific. Opinion, as elicited and expressed by two large and respectable conventions lately assembled at St. Louis and Memphis, points to a railroad as that which, if practicable, will best meet the wishes and wants of the country. But while this, if in successful operation, would be a work of great national importance and of a value to the country which it would be difficult to estimate, it ought also to be regarded as an undertaking of vast magnitude and expense, and one which must, if it be indeed practicable, encounter many difficulties in its construction and use. Therefore, to avoid failure and disappointment; to enable Congress to judge whether in the condition of the country through which it must pass the work be feasible, and, if it be found so, whether it should be undertaken as a national improvement or left to individual enterprise, and in the latter alternative what aid, if any, ought to be extended to it by the Government, I recommend as a preliminary measure a careful reconnoissance of the several proposed routes by a scientific corps and a report as to the practicability of making such a road, with an estimate of the cost of its construction and support. . . .

Our Government is one of limited powers, and its successful administration eminently depends on the confinement of each of its coordinate branches within its own appropriate sphere. The first section of the Constituion ordains that —

> All legislative powers herein granted shall be vested in a Congress of the United States, which shall consist of a Senate and House of Representatives.

The Executive has authority to recommend (not to dictate) measures to Congress. Having performed that duty, the executive department of the Government can not rightfully control the decision of Congress on any subject of legislation until that decision shall have been officially submitted to the President for approval. The check provided by the Constitution in the clause conferring the qualified veto will never be exercised by me except in the cases contemplated by the fathers of the Republic. I view it as an extreme measure, to be resorted to only in extraordinary cases, as where it may become necessary to defend the executive against the encroachments of the legislative power or to prevent hasty and inconsiderate or unconstitutional legislation. By cautiously confining this remedy within the sphere prescribed to it in the cotemporaneous expositions of the framers of the Constitution, the will of the people, legitimately expressed on all subjects of legislation through their constitutional organs, the Senators and Representatives of the United States, will have its full effect. As indispensable to the preservation of our system of self-government, the independence of the representatives of the States and the people is guaranteed by the Constitution, and they owe no responsibility to any human power but their constituents. By holding the representative responsible only to the people, and exempting him from all other influences, we elevate the nharacter of the constituent and quicken his sense of responsibility to his country. It is under these circumstances only that the elector can feel that in the choice of the lawmaker he is himself truly a component part of the sovereign power of the nation. With equal care we should study to defend the rights of the executive and judicial departments. Our Government can only be preserved in its purity by the suppression and entire elimination of every claim or tendency of one coordinate branch to encroachment upon another. With the strict observance of this rule and the other injunctions of the Constitution, with a sedulous inculcation of that respect and love for the Union of the States which our fathers cherished and enjoined upon their children, and with the aid of that overruling Providence which has so long and so kindly guarded our liberties and institutions, we may reasonably expect to transmit them, with their innumerable blessings, to the remotest posterity.

But attachment to the Union of the States should be habitually fostered in every American heart. For more than half a century, during which kingdoms and empires have fallen, this Union has stood unshaken. The patriots who formed it have long since descended to the grave; yet still it remains, the proudest monument to their memory and the object of affection and admiration with everyone worthy to bear the American name. In my judgment its dissolution would be the greatest of calamities, and to avert that should be the study of every American. Upon its preservation must depend our own happiness and that of countless generations to come. Whatever dangers may threaten it, I shall stand by it and maintain it in its integrity to the full extent of the obligations imposed and the powers conferred upon me by the Constitution

MESSAGE TO SENATE*
January 23, 1850

Sectional bitterness had already erupted when President Taylor sent this message to the Senate. Southern congressmen had expressed dire misgivings as to President Taylor's maneuverings in attempting to secure California as a free state. Talk of secession had taken place, and the President was anxious to clarify his role with relation to California and New Mexico. Personally affronted by attacks on his character, Taylor hoped the message would help to cool firery sentiment.

Texas, too, had rattled her sabers, and claimed a portion of New Mexican lands. The President attempted to conceal his agitation under the general heading of peaceful adjudication; privately, he spoke of using federal troops to quell Texas nationalism.

To the Senate of the United States

I transmit to the Senate, in answer to a resolution of that body passed on the 17th instant, the accompanying reports of heads of Departments which contain all the official information in the possession of the Executive asked for by the resolution.

On coming into office I found the military commandant of the Department of California exercising the functions of civil governor in that Territory and left, as I was, to act under the treaty of Guadalupe Hidalgo, without the aid of any legislative provision establishing a government in that Territory, I thought it best not to disturb that arrangement, made under my predecessor, until Congress should take some action on that subject. I therefore did not interfere with the powers of the military commandant, who continued to exercise the functions of civil governor as before; but I made no such appointment, conferred no such authority, and have allowed no increased compensation to the commandant for his services.

With a view to the faithful execution of the treaty so far as lay in the power of the Executive, and to enable Congress to act at the present session with as full knowledge and as little difficulty as possible on all matters of interest in these Territories, I sent the Hon. Thomas Butler King as bearer of dispatches to California, and certain officers to California and New Mexico, whose duties are particularly defined in the accompanying letters of instruction addressed to them severally by the proper Departments.

I did not hesitate to express to the people of those Territories my desire that each Territory should, if prepared to comply with the

---

*James Richardson, ed. *Messages and Papers of the Presidents*, Vol. 6, New York, 1897, pp. 2564–2568.

requisitions of the Constitution of the United States, form a plan of a State constitution and submit the same to Congress with a prayer for admission into the Union as a State, but I did not anticipate, suggest, or authorize the establishment of any such government without the assent of Congress, nor did I authorize any Government agent or officer to interfere with or exercise my influence or control over the election of delegates or over any convention in making or modifying their domestic institutions or any of the provisions of their proposed constitution. On the contrary, the instructions given by my orders were that all measures of domestic policy adopted by the people of California must originate solely with themselves; that while the Executive of the United States was desirous to protect them in the formation of any government republican in its character, to be at the proper time submitted to Congress, yet it was to be distinctly understood that the plan of such a government must at the same time be the result of their own deliberate choice and originate with themselves, without the interference of the Executive.

I am unable to give any information as to laws passed by any supposed government in California or of any census taken in either of the Territories mentioned in the resolution, as I have no information on those subjects.

As already stated, I have not disturbed the arrangements which I found had existed under my predecessor.

In advising an early application by the people of these Territories for submission as States I was actuated principally by an earnest desire to afford to the wisdom and patriotism of Congress the opportunity of avoiding occasions of bitter and angry dissensions among the people of the United States.

Under the Constitution every State has the right of establishing and from time to time altering its municipal laws and domestic institutions independently of every other State and of the General Government, subject only to the prohibitions and guaranties expressly set forth in the Constitution of the United States. The subjects thus left exclusively to the respective States were not designed or expected to become topics of national agitation. Still, as under the Constitution Congress has power to make all needful rules and regulations respecting the Territories of the United States, every new acquisition of territory has led to discussions on the question whether the system of involuntary servitude which prevails in may of the States should or should not be prohibited in that territory. The periods of excitement from this cause which have heretofore occurred have been safely passed, but during the interval, of whatever length, which may elapse before the admission of the Territories ceded by Mexico as States it appears probable that similar excitement will prevail to an undue extent.

Under these circumstances I thought, and still think, that it was my duty to endeavor to put it in the power of Congress, by the admission of California and New Mexico as States, to remove all occasion for the unnecessary agitation of the public mind.

It is understood that the people of the western part of California have formed a plan of a State constitution and will soon submit the same to the judgment of Congress and apply for admission as a State. This course on their part, though in accordance with, was not adopted exclusively in consequence of, any expression of my wishes, inasmuch as measures tending to this end had been promoted by the officers sent there by my predecessor, and were already in active progress of execution before any communication from me reached California. If the proposed constitution shall, when submitted to Congress, be found to be in compliance with the requisitions of the Constitution of the United States, I earnestly recommend that it may receive the sanction of Congress.

The part of California not included in the proposed State of that name is believed to be uninhabited, except in a settlement of our countrymen in the vicinity of Salt Lake.

A claim has been advanced by the State of Texas to a very large portion of the most populous district of the Territory commonly designated by the name of New Mexico. If the people of New Mexico had formed a plan of a State government for that Territory as ceded by the treaty of Guadalupe Hidalgo, and had been admitted by Congress as a State, our Constitution would have afforded the means of obtaining an adjustment of the question of boundary with Texas by a judicial decision. At present, however, no judicial tribunal has the power of deciding that question, and it remains for Congress to devise some mode for its adjustment. Meanwhile I submit to Congress the question whether it would be expedient before such adjustment to establish a Territorial government, which by including the district so claimed practically decide the question adversely to the State of Texas, or by excluding it would decide it in her favor. In my opinion such a course would not be expedient, especially as the people of this Territory still enjoy the benefit and protection of their municipal laws originally derived from Mexico and have a military force stationed there to protect them against the Indians. It is undoubtedly true that the property, lives, liberties, and religion of the people of New Mexico are better protected than they ever were before the treaty of cession.

Should Congress, when California shall present herself for incorporation into the Union, annex a condition to her admission as a State affecting her domestic institutions contrary to the wishes of her people, and even compel her temporarily to comply with it, yet the State could change her constitution at any time after admission when to her it should seem expedient. Any attempt to deny to the people of the State the right of self-government in a matter which peculiarly affects themselves will infallibly be regarded by them as an invasion of their rights, and, upon principles laid down in our own Declaration of Independence, they will certainly be sustained by the great mass of the American people. To assert that they are a conquered people and must as a State submit to the wukk of their conquerors in this regard will meet with no cordial response among American freemen. Great numbers of them are native citizens of the United States, not inferior to the rest of our countrymen in intelligence and patriotism, and no language of menace to restrain them in the exercise of an undoubted right, substantially guaranteed to them by the treaty of cession itself, shall ever be uttered by me or encouraged and sustained by persons acting under my authority. It is to be expected that in the residue of the territory ceded to us by Mexico the people residing there will at the time of their incorporation into the Union as a State settle all questions of domestic policy to suity themselves.

No material inconvenience will result from the want for a short period of a government established by Congress over that part of the territory which lies eastward of the new State of California; and the reasons for my opinion that New Mexico will at no very distant period ask for admission into the Union are founded on unofficial information which, I suppose, is common to all who have cared to make inquiries on that subject.

Seeing, then, that the question which now excites such painful sensations in the country will in the end certainly be settled by the silent effect of causes independent of the action of Congress, I again submit to your wisdom the policy recommended in my annual message of awaiting the salutary operation of those causes, believing that we shall thus avoid the creation of geographical parties and secure the harmony of feeling so necessary to the beneficial action of our political system. Connected, as the Union is, with the remembrance of past happiness, the sense of present blessings, and the hope of future peace and prosperity, every dictate of wisdom, every feeling of duty, and every emotion of patriotism tend to inspire fidelity and devotion to it and admonish us cautiously to avoid any unnecessary controversy which can either endanger it or impair ets strength, the chief element of which is to be found in the regard and affection of the people for each other.

MESSAGE TO THE SENATE
CONCERNING HUNGARY*
March 28, 1850

*While recognizing the aims of the Kossuth-led revolution-
ists in Hungary as basically democratic, President Taylor
wished to stress the difference between sympathy and
active support. The United States was not in a position
of strength to become embroiled in a foreign controversy,
one that might have had wide repercussions.*

To the Senate of the United States

In compliance with a resolution of the Senate of the 22nd instant, requesting the President of the United States to communicate to that body a copy of the instructions given to the agent of the United States who was employed to visit Hungary during the recent war between that country and Austria, and of the correspondence by and with such agent, so far as the publication of the same may be consistent with the public interest, I herewith transmit to the Senate a copy of the instructions to A. Dudley Mann, esq., relating to Hungary, he having been appointed by me special agent to that country on the 18th day of June last, together with a copy of the correspondence with our late charge d'affaires to Austria referred to in those instructions and of other papers disclosing the policy of this Government in reference to Hungary and her people. I also transmit, in compliance with the resolution of the Senate, but in a separate packet, a copy of the correspondence of Mr. Mann with the Department of State. The latter I have caused to be marked "executive" — the information contained in it being such as will be found on examination most appropriately to belong to the Senate in the exercise of its executive functions. The publication of this correspondence of the agent sent by me to Hungary is a matter referred entirely to the judgment and discretion of the Senate.

It will be seen by the documents now transmitted that no minister or agent was accredited by the Government of Hungary to this Government at any period since I came into office, nor was any communication ever received by this Government from the minister of foreign affairs of Hungary or any other executive officer authorized to act in her behalf.

My purpose, as freely avowed in this correspondence, was to have acknowledged the independence of Hungary had she succeeded in establishing a government de facto on a basis sufficiently permanent in its character to have justified me in doing so according to the usages and settled principles of this Government; and although she is now fal-

---

*James D. Richardson, ed. *The Messages and Papers of the Presidents.*
Vol. 6, New York, 1897, p. 2579.

len and many of her gallant patriots are in exile or in chains, I am free still to declare that had she been successful in the maintenance of such a government as we could have recognized we should have been the first to welcome her into the family of nations.

Z. TAYLOR

CLAYTON-BULWER TREATY*
April 19, 1850

Exhaustive sessions between Secretary of State John M. Clayton and Great Britain's Minister Plenipotentiary Sir Henry Lytton Bulwer eventually brought about an acceptable wording of the treaty that focused the attention of the American people to the isthmus of Central America and a future canal. President Taylor had confronted the negotiators on numerous occasions, and insisted on the right to understand every nuance inherent in the document. Although still disinclined to trust Great Britain, he rose from his sickbed to sign the treaty on July 5, 1850, the same day the treaty was passed by the Senate by a 42 to 10 vote. This proved to be the President's last official act, and he passed away four days later. The Clayton-Bulwer Treaty was abrogated by the Hay-Pauncefote Treaty in 1901.

CONVENTION BETWEEN THE UNITED STATES OF AMERICA AND HER BRITANNIC MAJESTY

The United States of America and Her Britannic Majesty, being desirous of consolidating the relations of amity which so happily subsist between them, by setting forth and fixing in a Convention their views and intentions with reference to any means of communication by Ship Canal, which may be constructed between the Atlantic and Pacific Ocean. — The President of the United States, has conferred full powers on John M. Clayton, Secretary of State of the United States; and Her Britannic Majesty on the Right Honorable Sir Henry Lytton Bulwer, a Member of the Most Honourable Order of the Bath, and Envoy Extraordinary and Minister Plenipotentiary of Her Britannic Majesty to the United States, for the aforesaid purpose; and the said Plenipotentiaries having exchanged their full powers, which were found to be in proper form, have agreed to the following articles.

ARTICLE 1.

The Governments of the United States and Great Britain hereby declare that neither the one nor the other will ever obtain or maintain for itself any exclusive control over the said Ship Canal; agreeing, that neither will ever erect or maintain any fortifications commanding the same, or in the vicinity thereof, or occupy, or fortify, or colonize, or assume, or exercise any dominion over Nicaragua, Costa

---

*Hunter Miller, ed. *Treaties and other International Acts of the United States of America.* Vol. 6, Washington, D.C., 1937, pp. 671–675.

Rica, the Mosquito Coast, or any part of Central America, nor will either make use of any protection which either affords or may afford, or any alliance which either has or may have, to or with any State or People for the purpose of erecting or maintaining any such fortifications, or of occupying, fortifying, or colonizing Nicaragua, Costa Rica, the Mosquito Coast or any part of Central America, or of assumming or exercising dominion over the same; nor will the United States or Great Britain take advantage of any intimacy, or use any alliance, connection or influence that either may possess with any State or Government through whose territory the said Canal may pass, for the purpose of acquiring or holding, directly or indirectly, for the citizens or subjects of the one, any rights or advantages in regard to commerce or navigation through the said Canal, which shall not be offered on the same terms to the citizens or subjects of the other.

ARTICLE II

Vessels of the United States or Great Britain, traversing the said Canal, shall, in case of war between the contracting parties, be exempted from blockade, detention or capture, by either of the belligerents; and this provision shall extend to such a distance from the two ends of the said Canal, as may hereafter be found expedient to establish.

ARTICLE III

In order to secure the construction of the said Canal, the contracting parties engage that, if any such Canal shall be undertaken upon fair and equitable terms by any parties having the authority of the local Government or Governments, through whose territory the same may pass, then the persons employed in making the said Canal and their property used, or to be used, for that object, shall be protected, from the commencement of the said Canal to its completion, by the Governments of the United States and Great Britain, from unjust detention, confiscation, seizure or any violence whatsoever.

ARTICLE IV

The contracting parties will use whatever influence they respectively exercise, with any State, States or Governments possessing, or claiming to possess, any jurisdiction or right over the territory which the said Canal shall traverse, or which shall be near the waters applicable thereto; in order to induce such States, or Governments, to facilitate the construction of the said Canal by every means in their Power: and furthermore, the United States and Great Britain agree to use their good offices, wherever or however it may be most expedient, in order to procure the establishment of two free Ports, – one at each end of the said Canal.

ARTICLE V

The contracting parties further engage that, when the said Canal shall have been completed, they will protect it from interruption, seizure or unjust confiscation, and that they will guarantee the neutrality thereof, so that the said Canal may forever be open and free, and the capital invested therein, secure. Nevertheless, the Governments of the United States and Great Britain, in according their protection to the construction of the said Canal, and guaranteeing its neutrality and security when completed, always understand that, this protection and guarantee are granted conditionally, and may be withdrawn by both Governments, or either Government, if both Governments, or either Government, should deem that the persons, or company, undertaking or managing the same, adopt or establish such regulations concerning the traffic thereupon, as are contrary to the spirit and intention of this Convention, − either by making unfair discriminations in favor of the commerce of one of the contracting parties over the commerce of the other, or by imposing oppressive exactions or unreasonable tolls upon passengers, vessels, goods, wares, merchandize or other articles. Neither party, however, shall withdraw the aforesaid protection and guarantee, without first giving six months notice to the other.

ARTICLE VI

The contracting parties in this Convention engage to invite every State with which both or either have friendly intercourse, to enter into stipulations with them similar to those which they have entered into with each other; to the end, that all other States may share in the honor and advantage of having contributed to a work of such general interest and importance as the Canal herein contemplated. And the contracting parties likewise agree that, each shall enter into Treaty stipulations with such of the Central American States, as they may deem advisable, for the purpose of more effectually carrying out the great design of this Convention, namely, − that of constructing and maintaining the said Canal as a ship−communication between the two Oceans for the benefit of mankind, on equal terms to all, and of protecting the same; and they, also, agree that, the good offices of either shall be employed, when requested by the other, in aiding and assisting the negotiation of such. Treaty stipulations; and, should any differences arise as to right or property over the territory through which the said Canal shall pass − between the States or Governments of Central America, − and such differences should, in any way, impede or obstruct the execution of the said Canal, the Governments of the United States and Great Britain will use their good offices to settle such differences in the manner best suited to promote the interests of the said Canal, and to strengthen the bonds of friendship and alliance which exist between the contracting parties.

ARTICLE VII

It being desirable that no time should be unnecessarily lost in commencing and constructing the said Canal, the Governments of the United States and Great Britain determine to give their support and encouragement to such persons, or company, as may first offer to commence the same with the necessary capital, the consent of the local authorities, and on such principles as accord with the spirit and intention of this Convention; and if any persons, or company, should already have, with any State through which the proposed Ship-Canal may pass, a contract for the construction of such a Canal as that specified in this Convention, — to the stipulations of which contract neither of the contracting parties in this Convention have any just cause to object, — and the said persons, or company, shall, moreover, have made preparations and expended time, money and trouble on the faith of such contract, it is hereby agreed, that such persons, or company, shall have a priority of claim over every other person, persons or company, to the protection of the Governments of the United States and Great Britain, and be allowed a year, from the date of the exchange of the ratifications of this Convention, for concluding their arrangements, and presenting evidence of sufficient capital subscribed to accomplish the contemplated undertaking; it being understood, that if, at the expiration of the aforesaid period, such persons, or company, be not able to commence and carry out the proposed enterprize, then the Governments of the United States and Great Britain shall be free to afford their protection to any other persons, or company, that shall be prepared to commence and proceed with the construction of the Canal in question.

ARTICLE VIII

The Governments of the United States and Great Britain having not only desired in entering into this Convention, to accomplish a particular object, but, also, to establish a general principle, they hereby agree to extend their protection, by Treaty stipulations, to any other practicable communications, whether by Canal or rail-way, across the Isthmus which connects North and South America; and especially, to the interoceanic communications, — should the same prove to be practicable, whether by Canal or rail-way, — which are now proposed to be established by the way of Tehuantepec, or Panama. In granting, however, their joint protection to any such Canals, or rail-ways, as are by this Article specified, it is always understood by the United States and Great Britain, that the parties constructing or owning the same, shall impose no other charges or conditions of traffic thereupon, than the aforesaid Governments shall approve, of, as just and equitable; and, that the same Canals, or rail-ways, being open to the citizens and subjects of the United States and Great Britain on equal terms, shall, also be open on like terms to the citizens and subjects of every other

State which is willing to grant thereto, such protection as the United States and Great Britain engage to afford.

ARTICLE IX

The ratifications of this Convention shall be exchanged at Washington, within six months from this day, or sooner, if possible.

In faith whereof, we, the respective Plenipotentiaries, have signed this Convention, and have hereunto affixed our Seals.

Done, at Washington, the nineteenth day of April, Anno Domini, one thousand eight hundred and fifty.

JOHN M. CLAYTON (Seal)
HENRY LYTTON BULWER (Seal)

ANNOUNCEMENT OF DEATH OF PRESIDENT TAYLOR*
July 9, 1850

The sudden death of President Zachary Taylor caused both consternation and excitement. Many advocates of compromise were assured that the new president, Millard Fillmore, would bridge the sectional dispute. Others feared that Fillmore would not have the personal attributes necessary to appeal to the nation's sense of union. Political sideliners were willing to sit back and watch the action.

DEATH OF PRESIDENT TAYLOR

Announcement to Mr. Fillmore

(From official records in the State Department)

DEPARTMENT OF STATE,
Washington, July 9, 1850

MILLARD FILLMORE,
      President of the United States

SIR: The melancholy and most painful duty devolves on us to announce to you that Zachary Taylor, late President of the United States is no more. He died at the President's Mansion this evening at half-past 10 o'clock.

We have the honor to be, etc.,

JOHN M. CLAYTON Secretary of State	GEO. W. CRAWFORD Secretary of War
W.M. MEREDITH Secretary of the Treasury	WM. BALLARD PRESTON Secretary of the Navy
T. EWING Secretary of the Interior	J. COLLAMER Postmaster-General

(The announcement as published in the Daily National Intelligencer of July 11, 1850, contains also the signature of Reverdy Johnson, Attorney-General.)

---

*James D. Richardson, ed. *Messages and Papers of the Presidents.* Vol. 6 New York, 1897, p. 2589.

CHRONOLOGY

EARLY LIFE AND CAREER

1800

January 7   Millard Fillmore, second of nine children born to Nathaniel and Phoebe Millard Fillmore, in Summerhill, Cayuga County, New York.

1815

Apprenticed to a cloth cutter. Fillmore's father was determined that his son would not pursue farming for his livelihood.

1817

An interest in books led Fillmore to purchase a share in a circulating library.

1819

Attended the Academy at New Hope, New York, where he fell in love with his teacher, Abigail Powers, who was two years older than her student. Abigail's father was a minister, and her brother was a local judge.

Served as a law clerk apprentice to County Judge Walter Wood for a short period of time.

1820

Taught elementary school for three months at Sempronius, New York, to earn money to further his law education. He returned to Judge Wood's employ.

1821

Left Judge Wood's law office and joined his father in Aurora, New York. His father had purchased farmland, hoping the new locale would improve his fortunes.

1821

Taught school in East Aurora, New York, and did some part-time legal work for the local justice of the peace.

1822

April   Taught school in the growing city of Buffalo, New York.

Returned to East Aurora to begin his own law practice, after having been designated a lawyer by the Court of Common Pleas in Buffalo.

1826

February 5   Married his former teacher Abigail Powers in her brother's home in Moravia, New York.

Admitted to act as an attorney in New York State's Supreme Court. His rapidly growing practice led him to take Nathan K. Hall, a friend, as a clerk.

1828

April 25   Son, Millard Powers Fillmore, born.

June   Delegate to Erie County's National Republican Convention. John Quincy Adams was chosen as the county's candidate for United States President. The National Convention, however, chose Henry Clay.

July   Attended Antimasonic Party caucus as a delegate from Erie County, New York.

September 25   Chosen as candidate of the Anti-Mason Party for a seat in New York's State Assembly.

November 13   Won a seat as New York State Assemblyman from Erie County. He served on unimportant committees during his first term in office.

1829

November   Reelected to New York State Assembly. By the end
                  of his second term in office, Fillmore was judged
                  a party leader.

1830

April   Moved to Buffalo, New York, where he and his wife
                  were active in the movement for the improvement
                  and expansion of public education, for an adequate
                  public library system, and for cultural and intel-
                  lectual enrichment. Their home library was a local
                  attraction.

November   Elected to third term as New York State Assembly-
                  man, a member of the National Republican Party,
                  the minority party in the Assembly. He was respon-
                  sible for the introduction and passage of two impor-
                  tant laws for the state; the first, eliminating im-
                  prisonment for debt, the second, the imposition of
                  a bankruptcy law to protect small business interests.
                  Fillmore's image had become a man "of the people."

1831

September 26   National Convention of Anti-Masons held in Baltimore,
                  Maryland. This was the first national nominating
                  convention in United States history. William Wirt
                  was chosen as the Presidential candidate, and Amos
                  Ellmacer for Vice President.

November   Joined the Unitarian Church, the first church joined
                  by Fillmore, although his wife had been raised in the
                  Baptist faith.

1832

March 27   Daughter, Mary Abigail Fillmore, born.

November   Elected as a National Republican to the United States
                  Congress from Buffalo, New York. Formed law part-
                  nership with Nathan K. Hall before leaving for Wash-
                  ington, D.C. Solomon G. Haven joined the firm a

1832

few years later, and the association of lawyers became widely known as the best in western New York.

CONGRESSMAN

December 2   Took his seat in United States House of Representatives and was known as an Anti-Mason thinker
within the National Republican fold. His beliefs
bridged the gap between the two political groups, and
eventually became the nucleus of the Whig Party.

The reelection of President Andrew Jackson had recently occurred, and Fillmore found himself part of
the United States Bank controversy. He was strongly
opposed to bank monopoly and doubted the value of
any banking system, state or federal.

1834

February 2   James W. Webb, editor of the New York Courier and
Inquirer, proposed that the anti-Jackson politicians
be known as Whigs. The first Whig candidates ran
in New York City, and were elected to the New York
City Council.

President Andrew Jackson's veto of the bill to recharter the U.S. Bank increased the tensions within
the factions of the Democratic Party, and many party
men left the Jacksonian ranks and became ardent con-
verts to the anti-Jackson Whig Party.

April   Anti-Mason Party leaders agreed to end the Party's
existence, and merge with other anti-Jackson groups
within the Whig Party.

July   Fillmore announced his affiliation as a member of
the Whig Party, and lost Antimasonic support from
his New York State constituency; he chose not to run
as a candidate of either party in the forthcoming elections.

1834

September   New York State Senator William Henry Seward ran as the first Whig candidate for the governorship of New York; he lost by a large majority to the Democratic incumbant William Marcy. The Whig Party, however, had elected many governors in other states.

December   Returned to private life in Buffalo, New York. He dedicated himself to forming a truly national Whig Party.

1835

October   Vehemently defended the rights of small landowners in western New York State, and, because of his defense, led hundreds of Antimasons to the Whig Party.

1836

August   Agreed to accept the Whig nomination for United States Congressman from Erie County, New York.

December 7   Fillmore elected to Congress. Former Democratic Vice President Martin Van Buren was elected President.

1837

September   The economic depression caused many hardships throughout the nation, and the Whig Party enjoyed the fruits of the discredited Democratic administration. Fillmore blamed the entire economic situation on Jackson's support of state banks and Nicholas Biddle's attempts to secure the continuation of the U.S. Bank.

December 28   British burned the American steamboat, the Caroline, which had been used to provide military supplies to a group of militant Canadians, who were attempting to "liberate" Canada. The public pressure for war on Britain was so great that President Van Buren issued a statement of neutrality (January, 1838).

1838

September   Supported William H. Seward for Governorship of
                        New York, even though he disliked the political ma-
                        nipulations of Thurlow Weed, Whig Party boss of
                        New York State.

December 3   William H. Seward elected governor of New York
                        State, an important victory for the new Whig Party.
                        The Party also took control of the United States House
                        of Representatives; Fillmore was reelected for a
                        third term to Congress.

December   Refused the offer of New York State Comptroller, a
                        lucrative position that fell under the patronage con-
                        trol of Thurlow Weed. Fillmore did not want to be
                        indebted in any way to Weed.

1839

December 4   Took an active interest in the Whig National Con-
                        vention, meeting in Harrisburg, Pennsylvania. The
                        convention chose William Henry Harrison of Ohio
                        as its candidate for President. John Tyler of Vir-
                        ginia was the Party's choice for Vice President.
                        "Tippecanoe and Tyler too" became the cry for a
                        Whig victory to bring Jacksonian politics to an end.

1840

March   Served as Chairman of the House Election Committee
                        which investigated the election of five Whig Congress-
                        men from New Jersey, who had been accused by the
                        Democratic Party of fraudulent activities. The
                        charges held under investigation, and the loss of the
                        five Whig seats gave the Democrats control of the
                        House.

December 2   William Henry Harrison elected first Whig President
                        of the United States. The Whigs also won a majority
                        in both Houses of Congress, and twelve governor-
                        ships. Fillmore was reelected to the House by a
                        large margin.

1841

April 4
After one month in office President William Henry Harrison died from pneumonia, ending the shortest term as President in American history. Vice President John Tyler assumed office. The Whig interests had a plan to cure the economic depression, which included the reestablishment of the U.S. Bank, and a bill had passed to insure that this be done. Tyler vetoed the bill, and completely alienated himself from the Whig leadership.

Fillmore was not a supporter of the U.S. Bank, and had unsuccessfully attempted to force compromise with the President and Congress.

July
Favored the increase of the U.S. tariff by 20 percent as a means for raising revenue for the U.S. Treasury, and as Chairman of the House Ways and Means Committee, saw the bill through until its final passage as law. Fillmore also suggested giving funds from public land sales directly to the states, thus avoiding political interests; this, too, became law.

August
President Tyler vetoed a second bill to recharter the U.S. Bank. Fillmore regretted that both Congress and the President were reluctant to settle their differences.

September 11
With the exception of Secretary of State Daniel Webster, all members of President Tyler's cabinet resigned in protest against Tyler's refusal to recharter the U.S. Bank.

September 15
The leadership of the Whig Party distributed a leaflet announcing the elimination of President Tyler from membership in the Party. Fillmore reluctantly supported the Party in its action.

1842

March 30
U.S. tariff increased to level of 1832, which was about a 30% level. Fillmore was the author and chief proponent of this legislation.

1842

July   Fillmore rejected the Whig renomination for Congress to return to New York to try and mend the broken fences in the Whig Party.

1843

October   Editor Horace Greeley, in the New York Tribune, supported Fillmore for the Vice Presidency in the coming election.

1844

May   Unsuccessful candidate for Vice President at the Whig National Convention. Theodore Frelinghuysen of New Jersey won the nomination and ran with Henry Clay, the Whig Presidential candidate. Fillmore's anti-slave beliefs led many to think of him as anti-southern, and he had already announced his opposition to Texas annexation.

July   Nominated by acclamation for Governor of New York. Samuel J. Wilkins ran as Fillmore's lieutenant-governor.

October 7   Defeated for the governorship of New York, along with the rest of the Whig ticket. Fillmore lost heavily in the urban areas, where his firm belief in separation of church and state turned many Roman Catholic voters against him.

1845-1846

Practiced law in Buffalo, but remained actively opposed to President Polk's policies, especially the Mexican War, which he saw as a means to weaken northern economic interests, and a southern attempt to spread slavery.

1846

Made honorary chancellor of the University of Buffalo, a position he held until his death.

1847

September   Decided to return to public life, and ran for Comp-
                   troller of New York.

November 10   Elected Comptroller of New York State, easily de-
                   feating Azariah C. Flagg, the Democratic candidate.

December   Moved to Albany to assume duties as New York State
                   Comptroller.

1848

March   Thurlow Weed, Whig political "boss" of New York,
                   suggested the names of William H. Seward and Abbott
                   Lawrence as nominees for Vice President to run with
                   General Zachary Taylor in the coming presidential
                   election.

June 7-9   Whig National Convention (See details under President
                   Taylor in this volume)

June 11   After the selection of General Zachary Taylor to run
                   for the Presidency, the Whig Convention delegates
                   looked for a northerner to balance the southren slave-
                   owning candidate. Fillmore's name was suddenly pro-
                   posed by John A. Collier, a delegate from New York,
                   to be the Party's choice for Vice President. The only
                   opposition to Fillmore was Abbott Lawrence. Fill-
                   more, however, more than doubled Lawrence's votes
                   on the second ballot.

June-November   Campaigned actively and made known his personal dis-
                   taste for slavery, but stated that only the states had
                   the right to regulate the "peculiar institution." He
                   ignored questions related to the problem of how the
                   newly acquired western lands should enter the Union
                   and rejected Congressional jurisdiction over state af-
                   fairs.

November 7   Elected Vice President of the United States. (For
                   specifics see entry under Zachary Taylor in this vol-
                   ume).

1849

February   William H. Seward elected to U.S. Senate from New
York; for the sake of Party Unity, Fillmore had supported Seward.

VICE PRESIDENT

March 5   Took Vice-Presidential oath of office in the Senate
chambers. A short speech was given extolling the
meaning of Union and his belief in democratic pro-
cesses.

January-June   Senator William H. Seward and his mentor, Thurlow
Weed, persuaded President Zachary Taylor that all
federal patronage in New York State should be distributed through them and Hamilton Fish, the Whig
governor of New York. Fillmore was left without a
voice in promoting men he felt most qualified to hold
patronage positions.

1850

January-June   As President of the Senate, presided throughout the
momentous debate that took place leading, eventually,
to the Compromise of 1850. Fillmore did not approve
of the President's stand against compromise, but refrained from voicing any opinion and appeared to support the administration.

July 9   Informed by a messenger that President Zachary Taylor was dead. Fillmore had expected the news and
had spent most of the day at the White House consoling
Taylor's family in the President's last hours.

PRESIDENT

July 10   Inaugurated President of the United States, at noon,
before a joint session of Congress. Judge Branch,
District Court jurist, administered the oath of office.

1850

July 17   Daniel Webster advised the President that the Senate
                    would agree to consider the various compromise pro-
                    posals separately.

August 8   Refused to be intimidated by Texas' threats of mili-
                    tary action against New Mexico. Senator James A.
                    Pearce of Maryland, a spokesman for Fillmore, con-
                    vinced a majority of Senators to pass a bill restricting
                    Texas from its present boundaries. After settling
                    the Texas problem, the House and Senate concentrated
                    on the bills collectively known as the "Compromise
                    of 1850."

                    The various bills made law by the President's signa-
                    ture were:

                    California admitted to the Union as a free state (Sep-
                    tember 9, 1850)

                    New Mexico to be organized as a territory, with no
                    restrictions on slavery, and Texas would be paid ten
                    million dollars for her agreement to accept the Texas-
                    New Mexican boundary. The future of slavery would
                    be dediced by the people of the territory. (September
                    9, 1850)

                    The Fugitive Slave Act was given additional strength
                    by giving the federal government complete jurisdiction
                    over all runaway slaves. Federal commissioners
                    would enforce the law by carrying out the arrest of
                    fugitive slaves, and the federal government would
                    punish any who hindered the action of the authorities.
                    (September 18, 1850)

                    Slave trade in the District of Columbia was abolished.
                    (September 20, 1850)

                    President Fillmore disliked the Fugitive Slave pro-

1850

vision, but believed it to be firmly on constitutional
grounds. He realized he was splitting his own Whig
Party by signing the bill.

October   At the New York State Whig nominating convention,
the Fillmore-Weed-Seward antagonisms found public
expression. A Seward-Weed resolution was passed
that stated disapproval of the Compromise of 1850.
The Fillmore contingent saw the resolution as a deliberate attempt to discredit the administration and
to swing the Whig Party to a free soil direction.

Fillmore was concerned that the New York Whig
division presaged a national split in the Party and
would lead to a third party movement. The President
backed the candidacy of Washington Hunt for New
York's governor, and Hunt narrowly won the election.
For the moment, the New York Whigs supported the
Fillmore administration.

Aroused the wrath of the abolitionists when he approved the use of federal military forces to assist
federal marshals in arresting fugitive slaves.

Reacted to threatened seizure of federal property by
inflamed Charlestonians by reinforcing federal troops
in that South Carolina city. Southern hostility had
been generated by the refusal of some northern states
to obey the Fugitive Slave Law.

November 12   Second Nashville Convention of southern statesmen
met to consider aspects of the Compromise of 1850.
Although talk of secession preceded the meeting, a
moderate opinion prevailed, and general acceptance
of the Compromise was recorded.

1851

March 1   Ex-governor Hamilton Fish of New York won a seat
in the United States Senate by one vote in the New York
State legislature. Fish's election was a victory for
the Thurlow Weed machine.

1851

July   Refused to take a stand in a dispute between United
              States businessmen and Mexico over a proposed rail-
              way route in southern Mexico.

August 3   Narcisco Lopez, an adventurer, launched a filibus-
              tering expedition of 400 southern men from New Or-
              leans to "liberate" Cuba from Spain. About one hun-
              dred American prisoners were jailed in Spain. Fill-
              more refused to support any sympathetic action on
              behalf of the American force and warned that he would
              not tolerate any further southern expeditions against
              the wishes of the government.

October   Assured England and France that the United States
              had no plans to acquire Cuba, but made it clear that
              any attempt by England or France to control Cuba
              would not be tolerated.

November   The Whig Party suffered many state election losses
              throughout the country. The American Democratic
              Party (formerly Native-American) and the Order of
              the Star-Spangled Banner appeared to be gathering
              Whigs into their respective political pens.

December 7   Suggested to political friends that he did not wish to
              run for reelection in 1852. He was implored, how-
              ever, to reconsider.

              Visited Henry Clay, who was very ill. Clay had an-
              nounced his support of Fillmore for the coming elec-
              tion.

1852

May   Decided to leave his name in the running as the Whig
              Presidential candidate, after having been convinced
              that Senator William Seward was attempting to create
              a new party with Whig supporters.

1852

June 1   Franklin Pierce of New Hampshire was chosen presidential candidate by the Democratic Party and William R. King of Alabama was chosen the Vice Presidential candidate.

June 16-24   Whig National Convention met in Baltimore, Maryland. Senator William Seward arrived early to press for the nomination of General Winfield S. Scott. Thurlow Weed also favored Scott. Daniel Webster, the Secretary of State, was also considered a favorite for the nomination, but was in poor health. Fillmore's supporters were led by his friend George Babcock of Buffalo.

The nomination for President required 147 votes. On the first roll call, Fillmore led with 133 votes, with Winfield S. Scott second with 131. Daniel Webster received 29 votes. Most of the President's support came from the South.

Webster's delegates remained loyal and refused to relinquish their votes to Fillmore. Webster, however, after three days and forty-six ballots, agreed to surrender his votes to Fillmore. On the 47th ballot, however, even with Webster's support, the tide turned from the President to General Scott. Scott won the nomination on the 53rd ballot.

William A. Graham of North Carolina, Fillmore's Secretary of Navy, was chosen Vice-Presidential candidate.

The results of the convention caused widespread consternation, especially in the South, and many politicians prophesized the imminent collapse of the Whig Party.

August 11   Convention of the Free Soil Party in Pittsburgh, Pennsylvania, nominated John P. Hale of New Hampshire

1852

for President and George W. Julien of Indiana for Vice President. The Free Soil platform opposed slavery, the further spread of slavery, and the Compromise of 1850.

October 24   Daniel Webster, Secretary of State, died at his home in Marshfield, Massachusetts.

November 2   Franklin Pierce, the Democratic candidate, elected 14th President of the United States, with 254 electoral votes from twenty-seven states. Winfield S. Scott, the Whig candidate, received 42 electoral votes from four states.

The election returns mirrored the split in the Whig Party; all the southern states (except Kentucky and Tennesses) voted for Pierce. The Whig Party appeared to be dead.

November 19   Commodore Matthew C. Perry received instructions to proceed to Japan with a fleet of four warships. Fillmore was most anxious to link the Japanese Islands to the United States trade route via San Francisco, Hawaii, and Shanghai.

December 6   Delivered his last Annual Message to Congress.

KNOW-NOTHING CANDIDATE

1853

March 4   Accompanied Franklin Pierce, in rain and snow, to the Inaugural ceremonies. He listened to the new President proclaim his allegiance to the Compromise of 1850 and extol the cause of Union.

March 5   Revised plans to leave Washington, D.C., because of Mrs. Fillmore's sudden illness. The President's wife had not been well before the Inaugural ceremonies but had insisted she attend.

1853

March 30   After three weeks of illness, Mrs. Fillmore died, still in residence at Willard's Hotel in Washington.

April 1   Mrs. Millard Fillmore buried in Buffalo, New York.

1854

January 4   Senator Stephen A. Douglas of Illinois presented a bill for the opening of Kansas and Nebraska territories for settlement and for popular sovereignty on the issue of slavery, thus repudiating the Missouri Compromise.

March 4   Kansas-Nebraska bill passed in Senate, 37-14.

March-June   Angered by the Kansas-Nebraska bill, Fillmore left his retirement and toured the country voicing his opposition. Especially galling to the ex-President was the memory of many years in office spent to prevent such an occurrence from happening.

May 30   Kansas-Nebraska bill signed into law by President Pierce.

June   The American Party founded in New York City. Convinced that the Roman Church was dedicated to a takeover of the American nation, all members of the Party swore to vote only for non-Catholics, and, if serving as an elected official, to remove Roman Catholics from boards and agencies. The members of the party were referred to as "Know-Nothings" by the general public because of the refusal of its members to reveal their activities.

Fillmore began to think in terms of making the American (Know-Nothing) Party a haven for disaffected Whigs. Neither approving or disapproving the nativist tenets of the Know-Nothings, Fillmore's main thought was directed to a national party, attractive to both North and South.

1854

July 26   Mary Abigail Fillmore, Fillmore's daughter, died
                 suddenly at the age of twenty-two. The shock of her
                 passing might have contributed to the ex-President's
                 decision to consider running for the Presidency on
                 the Know-Nothing ticket.

November   The national election returns reflected the rising
                 strength of the Know-Nothing Party in many northern
                 and southern states; this was especially so in former
                 Whig territory.

1855

January 1   In a letter to Know-Nothing Party leaders, Fillmore
                 made known his wishes to become the Presidential
                 candidate.

March   Left by steamship for a twelve months' European-
                 Levantine vacation. He visited many countries and
                 was entertained wherever he appeared, including a
                 reception by Queen Victoria.

                 In France, Fillmore provided personal financial aid
                 for the release of Horace Greeley, the editor of the
                 New York Tribune, who had been jailed in Paris for
                 debt.

1856

February 22   Although still on his European vacation, Fillmore
                 was nominated for the Presidency by the American
                 (Know-Nothing) Party at its national convention in
                 Philadelphia. Andrew Donelson of Kentucky was the
                 Party's choice for Vice-President. The platform
                 strongly advocated curbs on immigration, and repu-
                 diated any attempts to prevent slavery in the new ter-
                 ritories.

June 22   Fillmore returned from Europe.

1856

June 23-29   While on the way to Buffalo, Fillmore made twenty-
                  seven speeches at various places. He never once
                  stated anything that could be construed as his being
                  "anti-Catholic." Fillmore's conflict with the Roman
                  Church was based on his complete opposition to any
                  weakening of the separation of church and state.

July-October   The Know-Nothing campaign lost much of its early
                  excitement as the people of the nation became more
                  "northern" or "southern" in their allegiance. Many
                  of Fillmore's supporters left him to vote for James
                  Buchanan, the Democratic candidate, in order to keep
                  John C. Fremont, the Republican candidate, from
                  winning the Presidency.

November 4   James Buchanan of Pennsylvania, the Democratic can-
                  didate, elected President of the United States, with
                  174 electoral votes. Fremont received 114 electoral
                  votes. Fillmore received 8 electoral votes from the
                  single state of Maryland.

1858

February 10   Married Mrs. Caroline C. McIntosh, the widow of
                  a Troy, New York, businessman. His new wife in-
                  herited a rather large estate, and Fillmore became
                  the administrator of his wife's interests. The couple
                  purchased a very large, imposing mansion in Buffalo
                  and created an "intellectual" and "social" center.

1861

February 16   Entertained the newly elected President, Abraham
                  Lincoln, when he arrived in Buffalo, New York, on
                  his journey to Washington, D.C.

April   Although distressed with the news of the Civil War,
                  Fillmore led rallies in Buffalo to support the Union.
                  He remained a harsh critic of the Republican Party;
                  he felt the Republicans had provoked the war.

1862

Elected first president of the Buffalo Historical Society. Held office until 1867.

1865

April

He was out of town following Lincoln's assassination, and, therefore, his home was not draped with black bunting. Fillmore was accused of "favoring" Lincoln's death and local extremists smeared his house with black paint. Later, Fillmore led an official delegation to honor the train bearing Lincoln's body as it passed on its way to Illinois.

1866

August

Entertained President Andrew Johnson in Buffalo as the President was taking his famous political "swing around the circle" by rail.

1874

March 8

Died at the age of seventy-four after suffering for two weeks from partial paralysis. His remains lie in Forest Lawn Cemetery, Buffalo, New York. His widow, Mrs. Caroline McIntosh Fillmore, died seven years later.

COMPROMISE OF 1850*
September 9-20, 1850

The following congressional acts (excerpted) combined to form what is known as the Compromise of 1850. President Fillmore, while serving as President of the Senate, had privately supported compromise, although he publicly supported the adament position against compromise taken by President Taylor. After Taylor's death, Fillmore lost little time in assisting congressional leaders in facilitating the passage of the bills.

I. *Settling the Texas Boundaries, adjusting Texas claims, and establishing a territorial government for New Mexico, September 9, 1850.*

II. *The Admission of California, September 9, 1850.*

III. *Territorial Government for Utah. September 9, 1850.*

IV. *An Amended Fugitive Slave Law. September 18, 1850.*

V. *Slave Trade Prohibited in the District of Columbia. September 20, 1850.*

I. Setting the Texas Boundaries, adjusting Texas claims, and establishing a Territorial government for New Mexico, September 9, 1850

Be it enacted by the Senate and House of Representatives of the United States of America in Congress assembled, That the following propositions shall be, and the same hereby are, offered to the State of Texas, which, when agreed to by the said State, in an act passed by the general assembly, shall be binding and obligatory upon the United States, and upon the said State of Texas: Provided, The said agreement by the said general assembly shall be given on or before the first day of December, eighteen hundred and fifty:

FIRST. The State of Texas will agree that her boundary on the north shall commence at the point at which the meridian of one hundred degrees west from Greenwich is intersected by the parallel of thirty-six degrees thirty minutes north latitude, and shall run from said point due west to the meridian of one hundred and three degrees west from Greenwich; thence her boundary shall run due south to the thirty-second degree of north latitude; thence on the said parallel

---

*Statutes at Large and Treaties of the United States of America. Vol. 9, Boston, 1851, pp. 446—468.

of thirty-two degrees of north latitude to the Rio Bravo del Norte, and thence with the channel of said river to the Gulf of Mexico.

SECOND. The State of Texas cedes to the United States all her claim to territory exterior to the limits and boundaries which she agrees to establish by the first article of this agreement.

THIRD. The State of Texas relinquishes all claim upon the United States for liability of the debts of Texas, and for compensation or indemnity for the surrender to the United States of her ships, forts, arsenals, custom-houses, cutom-house revenue, arms and munitions of war, and public buildings with their sites, which became the property of the United States at the time of the annexation.

FOURTH. The United States, in consideration of said establishment of boundaries, cession of claim to territory, and relinquishment of claims, will pay to the State of Texas the sum of ten millions of dollars in a stock bearing five per cent. interest, and redeemable at the end of fourteen years, the interest payable half-yearly at the treasury of the United States.

SEC. 2. And be it further enacted. That all that portion of the Territory of the United States bounded as follows: Beginning at a point in the Colorado River where the boundary line with the republic of Mexico crosses the same; thence eastwardly with the said boundary line to the Rio Grande; thence following the main channel of said river to the parallel of the thirty-second degree of north latitude; thence east with said degree to its intersection with the one hundred and third degree of longitude west of Greenwich; thence north with said degree of longitude to the parallel of thirty-eighth degree of north latitude; thence west with said parallel to the summit of the Sierra Madre; thence south with the crest of said mountains to the thirty-seventh parallel of north latitude; thence west with said parallel to its intersection with the boundary line of the State of California; thence with said boundary line to the place of beginning − be, and the same is hereby, erected into a temporary government, by the name of the Territory of New Mexico: Provided, That nothing in this act contained shall be construed to inhibit the government of the United States from dividing said Territory into two or more Territories, in such manner and at such times as Congress shall deem convenient and proper, or from attaching any portion thereof to any other Territory or State: And provided, further That, when admitted as a State, the said Territory, or any portion of the same, shall be received into the Union, with or without slavery, as their constitution may prescribe at the time of their admission.

SEC. 3. And be it further enacted, That the executive power and authority in and over said Territory of New Mexico shall be vested in a governor, who shall hold his office for four years, and until his successor shall be appointed and qualified, unless sooner removed by the President of the United States. . .

II. The Admission of California, September 9, 1850.

Whereas the people of California have presented a constitution and asked admission into the Union, which constitution was submitted to Congress by the President of the United States, by message dated February thirteenth, eighteen hundred and fifty, and which, on due examination, is found to be republican in its form of government.

Be it enacted by the Senate and House of Representatives of the United States of America in Congress assembled, That the State of California shall be one, and is hereby declared to be one, of the United States of America, and admitted into the Union on an equal footing with the original States in all respects whatever.

SEC. 2 And be it further enacted, That, until the representatives of Congress shall be apportioned according to an actual enumeration of the inhabitants of the United States, the State of California shall be entitled to two representatives in Congress.

SEC. 3. And be it further enacted, That the said State of California is admitted into the Union upon the express condition that the people of said State, through their legislature or otherwise, shall never interfere with the primary disposal of the public lands within its limits, and shall pass no law and do no act whereby the title of the United States to, and right to dispose of, the same shall be impaired or questioned and that they shall never lay any tax or assessment of any description whatsoever upon the public domain of the United States, and in no sense shall non-resident proprietors, who are citizens of the United States be taxed higher than residents; and that all the navigable waters within the said State shall be common highways, and forever free, as well to the inhabitants of said State as to the citizens of the United States, without any tax, impost, or duty therefor: Provided, That nothing herein contained shall be construed as recognizing or rejecting the propositions tendered by the people of California as articles of compact in the ordinance adopted by the convention which formed the constitution of that State.

Approved, September 9, 1850.

III. Territorial government for Utah, September 9, 1850.

Be it enacted by the Senate and House of Representatives of the United States of America in Congress assembled, That all that part of the territory of the United States included within the following limits, to wit: bounded on the west by the State of California, on the north by the Territory of Oregon, and on the east by the summit of the Rocky Mountains, and on the south by the thirty-seventh parallel of north latitude, be, and the same is hereby, created into a temporary of north latitude, be, and the same is hereby, created into a temporary government, by the name of the Territory of Utah; and, when admitted as a State, the said Territory, or any portion of the same, shall be received into the Union, with or without slavery, as their constitution may prescribe at the time of their admission: Provided, That nothing in this act contained shall be construed to inhibit the government of the United States from dividing said Territory into two or more Territories, in such manner and at such times as Congress shall deem convenient and proper, or from attaching any portion of said Territory to any other State or Territory of the United States.

IV. An amended Fugitive Slave Act, September 18, 1850

Be it enacted by the Senate and House of Representatives of the United States of America in congress assembled, That the persons who have been, or may hereafter be, appointed commissioners, in virtue of any act of Congress, by the Circuit Courts of the United States, and who, in consequence of such appointment, are authorized to exercise the powers that any justice of the peace, or other magistrate of any of the United States, may exercise in respect to offenders for any crime or offence against the United States, by arresting, imprisoning, or bailing the same under and by virtue of the thirty-third section of the act of the twenty-fourth of September seventeen hundred and eighty-nine, entitled ''An Act to establishing the judicial courts of the United States,'' shall be, and are hereby, authorized and required to exercise and discharge all the powers and duties conferred by this act.

SEC. 2. And be it further enacted, That the Superior Court of each organized Territory of the United States shall have the same power to appoint commissioners to take acknowledgements of bail and affidavits, and to take depositions of witnesses in civil causes, which is now possessed by the Circuit Court of the United States; and all commissioners who shall hereafter be appointed for such purposes by the Superior Court of any organized Territory of the United States, shall possess all the powers, and exercise all the duties, conferred by law upon the commissioners appointed by the Circuit Courts of the United States for similar purposes, and shall moreover exercise and discharge all the powers and duties conferred by this act.

SEC. 3. And be it further enacted, That the Circuit Courts of the United States, and the Superior Courts of each organized Territory of the United States, shall from time to time enlarge the number of commissioners, with a view to afford reasonable facilities to reclaim fugitives from labor, and to the prompt discharge of the duties imposed by this act.

SEC. 4. And be it further enacted, That the commissioners above named shall have concurrent jurisdiction with the judges of the Circuit and District Courts of the United States, in their respective circuits and districts within the several States, and the judges of the Superior Courts of the Territories, severally and collectively, term-time and vacation; and shall grant certificates to such claimants, upon satisfactory proof being made, with authority to take and remove such fugitives from service or labor, under the restrictions herein contained, to the State or Territory from which such persons may have escaped or fled.

SEC. 5 And be it further enacted, That it shall be the duty of all marshals and deputy marshals to obey and execute all warrants and precepts issued under the provisions of this act, when to them directed; and should any marshal or deputy marshal refuse to receive such warrant, or other process, when tendered, or to use all proper means diligently to execute the same, he shall, on conviction thereof, be fined in the sum of one thousand dollars, to the use of such claimant, on the motion of such claimant, by the Circuit or District Court for the district of such marshal; and after arrest of such fugitive, by such marshal or his deputy, or whilst at any time in his custody under the provisions of this act, should such fugitive escape, whether with or without the assent of such marshal or his deputy, such marshal shall be liable, on his official bond, to be prosecuted for the benefit of such claimant, for the full value of the service or labor of said fugitive in the State, Territory, or District whence he escaped: and the better to enable the said commissioners, when thus appointed, to execute their duties faithfully and efficiently, in conformity with the requirements of the Constitution of the United States and of this act, they are hereby authorized and empowered, within their counties respectively, to appoint, in writing under their hands, any one or more suitable persons, from time to time, to execute all such warrants and other process as may be issued by them in the lawful performance of their respective duties; with authority to such commissioners, or the persons to be appointed by them, to execute process as aforesaid, to summon and call to their aid the bystanders, or posse comitatus of the proper county, when necessary to ensure a faithful observance of the clause of the Constitution referred to, in conformity with the provisions of this act; and all good citizens are hereby commanded to aid and assist in the prompt and efficient execution of this law, whenever their services may be required, as aforesaid, for that purpose; and said warrants shall run, and be executed by said officers, any where in the State within which they are issued.

SEC. 6. And be it further enacted, That when a person held to service or labor in any State or Territory of the United States, has heretofore or shall hereafter escape into another State or Territory of the United States, the person to whom such service or labor may be due, or his, her, or their agent or attorney, duly authorized, by power of attorney, in writing, acknowledged and certified under the seal of some legal officer or court of the State or Territory in which the same may be executed, may pursue and reclaim such fugitive person, either by procurring a warrant from some one of the courts, judges, or commissioners aforesaid, of the proper circuit, district, or county, for the apprehension of such fugitive from service or labor, or by seizing and arresting such fugitive, where the same can be done without process, and by taking, or causing such person to be taken, forthwith before such court, judge, or commissioner, whose duty it shall be to hear and determine the case of such claimant in a summary manner; and upon satisfactory proof being made, by deposition or affidavit, in writing, to be taken and certified by such court, judge, or commissioner, or by other satisfactory testimony, duly taken and certified by some court, magistrate, justice of the peace, or other legal officer authorized to administer an oath and take depositions under the laws of the State or Territory from which such person owing service or labor may have escaped, with a certificate of such magistracy or other authority, as aforesaid, with the seal of the proper court or officer thereto attached, which seal shall be sufficient to establish the competency of the proof, and with proof, also by affidavit, of the identity of the person whose service or labor is claimed to be due as aforesaid, that the person so arrested does in fact owe service or labor to the person or persons claiming him or her, in the State or Territory from which such fugitive may have escaped as aforesaid, and that said person escaped, to make out and deliver to such claimant, his or her agent or attorney, a certificate setting forth the substantial facts as to the service or labor due from such fugitive to the claimant, and of his or her escape from the State or Territory in which such service or labor was due, to the State or Territory in which he or she was arrested, with authority to such claimant, or his or her agent or attorney, to use such reasonable force and restraint as may be necessary, under the circumstances of the case, to take and remove such fugitive person back to the State or Territory whence he or she may have escaped as aforesaid. In no trial or hearing under this act shall the testimony of such alleged fugitive be admitted in evidence; and the certificates in this and the first (fourth) section mentioned, shall be conclusive of the right of the person or persons in whose favor granted, to remove such fugitive to the State or Territory from which he escaped, and shall prevent all molestation of such person or persons by any process issued by any court, judge, magistrate, or other person whomsoever.

SEC. 7. And be it further enacted, That any person who shall knowingly and willingly obstruct, hinder, or prevent such claimant, his agent or attorney, or any person or persons lawfully assisting him, her, or them, from arresting such a fugitive from service or labor, either with or without process as aforesaid, when so arrested, pursuant to the authority herein given and declared; or shall aid, abet, or assist such person so owing service or labor as aforesaid, directly or indirectly, to escape from such claimant, his agent or attorney, or other person or persons legally authorized as aforesaid; or shall harbor or conceal such fugitive, so as to prevent the discovery and arrest of such person, after notice or knowledge of the fact that such person was a fugitive from service or labor as aforesaid, shall, for either of said offences, be subject to a fine not exceeding one thousand dollars, and imprisonment not exceeding six months, by indictment and conviction before the District Court of the United States for the district in which such offense may have been committed, or before the proper court of criminal jurisdiction, if committed within any one of the organized Territories of the United States; and shall moreover forfeit and pay, by way of civil damages to the party injured by such illegal conduct, the sum or one thousand dollars, for each fugitive so lost as aforesaid, to be recovered by action of debt, in any of the District or Territorial Courts aforesaid, within whose jurisdiction the said offence may have been committed. . . .

V. Slave Trade Prohibited in the District of Columbia, September 20, 1850

Be it enacted by the Senate and House of Representatives of the United States of America in Congress assembled, That from and after the first day of January, eighteen hundred and fifty-one, it shall not be lawful to bring into the District of Columbia any slave whatever, for the purpose of being sold, or for the purpose of being placed in depot, to be subsequently transferred to any other State or place to be sold as merchandize. And if any slave shall be brought into the said District by its owner, or by the authority or consent of its owner, contrary to the provisions of this act, such slave shall thereupon become liberated and free.

SEC. 2. And be it further enacted, That it shall and may be lawful for each of the corporations of the cities of Washington and George town, from time to time, and as often as may be necessary, to abate, break up, and abolish any depot or place of confinement of slaves brought into the said District as merchandize, contrarty to the provisions of this act, by such appropriate means as may appear to either of the said corporations expedient and proper. And the same power is hereby vested in the Levy Court of Washington county, if any attempt shall be made, within its jurisdictional limits, to establish a depot or place of confinement for slaves brought into the said District as merchandize for sale contrary to this act.

FIRST ANNUAL MESSAGE*
December 2, 1850

*President Fillmore's first address to Congress contains
frequent allusions to the proper respect due to federal law,
expecially as a protection for the majority of Americans.
The outcry in the North against the new Fugitive Slave
Act was giving Fillmore political and moral qualms; his
own Whig Party was seriously divided on the issue, and
Fillmore, himself, found the Fugitive Slave Act repulsive
but necessary for national peace.*

*The section on revision of the tariff from an ad valorum
imposition to a more uniform change reflects Fillmore's
long interest in creating an economic foundation favorable to the nation's industries.*

Fellow-Citizens of the Senate and of the House of Representatives:

Being suddenly called in the midst of the last session of Congress by
a painful dispensation of Divine Providence to the responsible station
which I now hold, I contented myself with such communications to the
Legislature as the exigency of the moment seemed to require. The
country was shrouded in mourning for the loss of its venerable Chief
Magistrate and all hearts were penetrated with grief. Neither the
time nor the occasion appeared to require or to justify on my part any
general expression of political opinions or any announcement of the
principles which would govern me in the discharge of the duties to the
performance of which I had been so unexpectedly called. I trust, therefore, that it may not be deemed inappropriate if I avail myself of this
opportunity of the reassembling of Congress to make known my sentiments in a general manner in regard to the policy which ought to be
pursued by the Government both in its intercourse with foreign nations
and its management and administration of internal affairs.

Nations, like individuals in a state of nature, are equal and independent, possessing certain rights and owing certain duties to each
other, arising from their necessary and unavoidable relations; which
rights and duties there is no common human authority to protect and
enforce. Still, they are rights and duties, binding in morals, in conscience, and in honor, although there is no tribunal to which an injured
party can appeal but the disinterested judgment of mankind, and ulti-
mately the arbitrament of the sword.

Among the acknowledged rights of nations is that which each pos-
sesses of establishing that form of government which it may deem most
conducive to the happiness and prosperity of its own citizens, of
changing that form as circumstances may require, and of managing its
internal affairs according to its own will. The people of the United

*James D. Richardson, ed. *The Messages and Papers of the Presidents*,
Vol. 6, New York, 1897, pp. 2580–2589.

States claim this right for themselves, and they readily concede it to others. Hence it becomes an imperative duty not to interfere in the government or internal policy of other nations; and although we may sympathize with the unfortunate or the oppressed everywhere in their struggles for freedom, our principles forbid us from taking any part in such foreign contests. We make no wars to promote or to prevent successions to thrones, to maintain any theory of a balance of power, or to suppress the actual government which any country chooses to establish for itself. We instigate no revolutions, nor suffer any hostile military expeditions to be fitted out in the United States to invade the territory or provinces of a friendly nation. The great law of morality ought to have a national as well as a personal and individual application. We should act toward other nations as we wish them to act toward us, and justice and conscience should form the rule of conduct between governments, instead of mere power, self interest, or the desire of aggrandizement. To maintain a strict neutrality in foreign wars, to cultivate friendly relations, to reciprocate every noble and generous act, and to perform punctually and scrupulously every treaty obligation − these are the duties which we owe to other states, and by the performance of which we best entitle ourselves to like treatment from them; or, if that, in any case, be refused, we can enforce our own rights with justice and a clear conscience.

In our domestic policy the Constitution will be my guide, and in questions of doubt I shall look for its interpretation to the judicial decisions of that tribunal which was established to expound it and to the usage of the Government, sanctioned by the acquiescence of the country. I regard all its provisions as equally binding. In all its parts it is the will of the people expressed in the most solemn form, and the constituted authorities are but agents to carry that will into effect. Every power which it has granted is to be exercised for the public good; but no pretense of utility, no honest conviction, even, of what might be expedient, can justify the assumption of any power not granted. The powers conferred upon the Government and their distribution to the several departments are as clearly expressed in that sacred instrument as the imperfection of human language will allow, and I deem it my first duty not to question its wisdom, add to its provisions, evade its requirements, or nullify its commands.

Upon you, fellow-citizens, as the representatives of the States and the people, is wisely devolved the legislative power. I shall comply with my duty in laying before you from time to time any information calculated to enable you to discharge your high and responsible trust for the benefit of our common constituents.

My opinions will be frankly expressed upon the leading subjects of legislation; and if − which I do not anticipate − any act should pass the two Houses of Congress which should appear to me unconstitutional, or an encroachment on the just powers of other departments, or with pro-

visions hastily adopted and likely to produce consequences injurious
and unforseen, I should not shrink from the duty of returning it to you,
with my reasons, for your further consideration. Beyond the due performance of these constitutional obligations, both my respect for the
Legislature and my sense of propriety will restrain me from any attempt to control or influence your proceedings. With you is the power,
the honor, and the responsibility of the legislation of the country.

The Government of the United States is a limited Government. It
is confined to the exercise of powers expressly granted and such
others as may be necessary for carrying those powers into effect; and
it is at all times an especial duty to guard against any infringement on
the just rights of the States. Over the objects and subjects intrusted to
Congress its legislative authority is supreme. But here that authority
ceases, and every citizen who truly loves the Constitution and desires
the continuance of its existence and its blessings will resolutely and
firmly resist any interference in those domestic affairs which the
Constitution has clearly and unequivocally left to the exclusive authority of the States. And every such citizen will also deprecate useless
irritation among the several members of the Union and all reproach
and crimination tending to alienate one portion of the country from
another. The beauty of our system of government consists, and its
safety and durability must consist, in avoiding mutual collisions and
encroachments and in the regular separate action of all, while each
is revolving in its own distinct orbit.

The Constitution has made it the duty of the President to take care
that the laws be faithfully executed. In a government like ours, in which
all laws are passed by a majority of the representatives of the people,
and these representatives are chosen for such short periods that any
injurious or obnoxious law can very soon be repealed, it would appear
unlikely that any great numbers hould be found ready to resist the execution of the laws. But it must be borne in mid that the country is extensive; that there may be local interests or prejudices rendering a
law odious in one part which is not so in another, and that the thoughtless and inconsiderate, misled by their passions or their imaginations,
may be induced madly to resist such laws as they disapprove. Such
persons should recollect that without law there can be no real practical
liberty; that when law is trampled under foot tyranny rules, whether
it appears in the form of a military despotism or of popular violence.
The law is the only sure protection of the weak and the only efficient
restraint upon the strong. When impartially and faithfully administered,
none is beneath its protection and none above its control. You, gentle-
men, and the country may be assured that to the utmost of my ability
and to the extent of the power vested in me I shall at all times and in
all places take care that the laws be faithfully executed. In the discharge of this duty, solemnly imposed upon me by the Constitution and
by my oath of office, I shall shrink from no responsibility, and shall

endeavor to meet events as they may arise with firmness, as well as with prudence and discretion.

The appointing power is one of the most delicate with which the Executive is invested. I regard it as a sacred trust, to be exercised with the sole view of advancing the prosperity and happiness of the people. It shall be my effort to elevate the standard of official employment by selecting for places of importance individuals fitted for the posts to which they are assigned by their known integrity, talents, and virtues. In so extensive a country, with so great a population, and where few persons appointed to office can be known to the appointing power, mistakes will sometimes unavoidably happen and unfortunate appointments be made notwithstanding the greatest care. In such cases the power of removal may be properly exercised; and neglect of duty or malfeasance in office will be no more tolerated in individuals appointed by myself than in those appointed by others. . . .

All experience has demonstrated the wisdom and policy of raising a large portion of revenue for the support of Government from duties on good imported. The power to lay these duties is unquestionable, and its chief object, of course, is to replenish the Treasury, But if in doing this an incidental advantage may be gained by encouraging the industry of our own citizens, it is our duty to avail ourselves of that advantage.

A duty laid upon an article which can not be produced in this country, such as tea or coffee, adds to the cost of the article, and is chiefly or wholly paid by the consumer. But a duty laid upon an article which may be produced here stimulates the skill and industry of our own country to produce the same article, which is brought into the market in competition with the foreign article, and the importer is thus compelled to reduce his price to that at which the domestic article can be sold, thereby throwing a part of the duty upon the producer of the foreign article. The continuance of this process creates the skill and invites the capital which finally enable us to produce the article much cheaper than it could have been procured from abroad, thereby benefiting both the producer and the consumer at home. The consequence of this is that the artisan and the agriculturist are brought together, each affords a ready market for the produce of the other, the whole country becomes prosperous, and the ability to produce every necessary of life renders us independent in war as well as in peace.

A high tariff can never be permanent. It will cause dissatisfaction, and will be changed. It excludes competition, and thereby invites the investment of capital in manufactures to such excess that when changed it brings distress, bankruptcy, and ruin upon all who have been misled by its faithless protection. What the manufacturer wants is uniformity and permanency, that he may feel a confidence that he is not to be ruined by sudden changes. But to make a tariff uniform and permanent it is not only necessary that the laws should not be altered but that the duty should not fluctuate. To effect this all duties should be specific wherever the nature of the article is such as to admit of it. Ad valorem duties fluctuate with the price and offer strong temptations to fraud and perjury. Specific duties, on the contrary, are equal and uniform in all ports and at all times, and offer a strong inducement to the importer to bring the best article, as he pays no more duty upon that than upon one of inferior quality. I therefore strongly recommend a modification of the present tariff, which has prostrated some of our most important and necessary manufactures, and that specific duties be imposed sufficient to raise the requisite revenue, making such discriminations in favor of the industrial pursuits of our own country as to encourage home production without excluding foreign competition. It is also important that an unfortunate provision in the present tariff, which imposes a much higher duty upon the raw material that enters into our manufactures than upon the manufactured article, should be remedied.

Texas and New Mexico are surrounded by powerful tribes of Indians, who are a source of constant terror and annoyance to the inhabitants. Separating into small predatory bands, and always mounted, they overrun the country, devastating farms, destroying crops, driving off whole herds of cattle, and occasionally murdering the inhabitants or carrying them into captivity. The great roads leading into the country are infested with them, whereby traveling is rendered extremely dangerous and immigration is almost entirely arrested. The Mexican frontier, which by the eleventh article of the treaty of Guadalupe Hidalgo we are bound to protect against the Indians within our border, is exposed to these incursions equally with our own. The military force stationed in that country, although forming a large proportion of the Army, is represented as entirely inadequate to our own protection and the fulfillment of our treaty stipulations with Mexico. The principal deficiency is in cavalry, and I recommend that Congress should, at as early a period as practicable, provide for the raising of one or more regiments of mounted men. . . .

The act, passed at your last session, making certain propositions to Texas for settling the disputed boundary between that State and the Territory of New Mexico was, immediately on its passage, transmitted by express to the governor of Texas, to be laid by him before the general assembly for its agreement thereto. Its receipt was duly acknowledged, but no official information has yet been received of the action of the general assembly thereon. It may, however, be very soon expected, as, by the terms of the propositions submitted they were to have been acted upon on or before the first day of the present month.

It was hardly to have been expected that the series of measures passed at your last session with the view of healing the sectional differences which had sprung from the slavery and territorial questions should at once have realized their beneficent purpose. All mutual concession in the nature of a compromise must necessarily be unwelcome to men of extreme opinions. And though without such concessions our

Constitution could not have been formed, and can not be permanently sustained, yet we have seen them made the subject of bitter controversy in both sections of the Republic. It required many months of discussion and deliberation to secure the concurrence of a majority of Congress in their favor. It would be strange if they had been received with immediate approbation by people and States prejudiced and heated by the exciting controversies of their representatives. I believe those measures to have been required by the circumstances and condition of the country. I believe they were necessary to allay asperities and animosities that were rapidly alienating one section of the country from another and destroying those fraternal sentiments which are the strongest supports of the Constitution. They were adopted in the spirit of conciliation and for the purpose of conciliation. I believe that a great majority of our fellowcitizens sympathize in that spirit and that purpose, and in the main approve and are prepared in all respects to sustain these enactments. I can not doubt that the American people, bound together by kindred blood and common traditions, still cherish a paramount regard for the Union of their fathers, and that they are ready to rebuke any attempt to violate its integrity, to disturb the compromises on which it is based, or to resist the laws which have been enacted under its authority.

The series of measures to which I have alluded are regarded by me as a settlement in principle and substance — a final settlement of the dangerous and exciting subjects which they embraced. Most of these subjects, indeed, are beyond your reach, as the legislation which disposed of them was in its character final and irrevocable. It may be presumed from the opposition which they all encountered that none of those measures was free from imperfections, but in their mutual dependence and connection they formed a system of compromise the most conciliatory and best for the entire country that could be obtained from conflicting sectional interests and opinions.

For this reason I recommend your adherence to the adjustment established by those measures until time and experience shall demonstrate the necessity of further legislation to guard against evasion or abuse.

By that adjustment we have been rescued from the wide and boundless agitation that surrounded us, and have a firm, distinct, and legal ground to rest upon. And the occasion, I trust, will justify me in exhorting my countrymen to rally upon and maintain that ground as the best, if not the only, means of restoring peace and quiet to the country and maintaining inviolate the integrity of the Union. . . .

PROCLAMATION ON VIOLENCE IN BOSTON*
March 15, 1851

*Intense feelings permeated in the nation as the Fugitive
Slave Act was enforced. In Boston, Massachusetts, the
center of abolitionism, a mob action on the person of a
federal marshal took place. President Fillmore issued this
forceful proclamation with the sincere but deluded hope
that the extremeism in both North and South would merge
to one of moderate respect for the law.*

Whereas information has been received that sundry lawless persons,
principally persons of color, combined and confederated together for
the purpose of opposing by force the execution of the laws of the United
States, did, at Boston, in Massachusetts, on the 15th of this month,
make a violent assault on the marshal or duputy marshals of the United
States for the district of Massachusetts, in the court house, and did
overcome the said officers, and did by force rescue from their custody a person arrested as a fugitive slave, and then and there a prisoner lawfully holden by the said marshal or deputy marshals of the
United States, and other scandalous outrages did commit in violation
of law:

Now, therefore, to the end that the authority of the laws may be
maintained and those concerned in violating them brought to immediate and condign punishment, I have issued this my proclamation, calling on all well-disposed citizens to rally to the support of the laws of
their country, and requiring and commanding all officers, civil and
military, and all other persons, civil or military, who shall be found
within the vicinity of this outrage, to be aiding and assisting by all
means in their power in quelling this and other such combinations and
assisting the marshal and his deputies in recapturing the above-
mentioned prisoner; and I do especially direct that prosecutions be
commenced against all persons who shall have made themselves aiders
or abettors in or to this flagitious offense; and I do further command
that the district attorney of the United States and all other persons
concerned in the administration or execution of the laws of the United
States cause the foregoing offenders and all such as aided, abetted, or
assisted them or shall be found to have harbored or concealed such
fugitive contrary to law to be immediately arrested and proceeded
with according to law.

---

*James D. Richardson, ed. *The Messages and Papers of the Presidents.*
Vol. 6, New York, 1897, pp. 2645–2646.

Given under my hand and the seal of the United States this 18th day
of February, 1851.

(Seal)   MILLARD FILLMORE

Danl. Webster,
    Secretary of State.

MESSAGE TO THE SENATE*
February 19, 1851

When a large group of Boston abolitionists mobbed a federal marshal in the act of arresting a fugitive slave, President Fillmore was extremely annoyed. Southern pressures on the executive office were always intense, and the President was placed in the position of either enforcing the law, or losing any Whig support he had left in Massachusetts. He chose to place the matter before the Senate, and gather what support he might get to overcome the civil disobedience. None was forthcoming, and the gap between the North and South widened.

I have received the resolution of the Senate of the 18th instant, requesting me to lay before that body, if not incompatible with the public interest, any information I may possess in regard to an alleged recent case of a forcible resistance to the execution of the laws of the United States in the city of Boston, and to communicate to the Senate, under the above conditions, what means I have adopted to meet the occurrence, and whether in my opinion any additional legislation is necessary to meet the exigency of the case and to move vigorously execute existing laws.

The public newspapers contain an affidavit of Patrick Riley, a deputy marshal for the district of Massachusetts, setting forth the circumstances of the case, a copy of which affidavit is herewith communicated. Private and unofficial communications concur in establishing the main facts of this account, but no satisfactory official information has as yet been received; and in some important respects the accuracy of the account has been denied by persons whom it implicates. Nothing could be more unexpected than that such a gross violation of law, such a high-handed contempt of the authority of the United States, should be perpetrated by a band of lawless confederates at noonday in the city of Boston, and in the very temple of justice. I regard this flagitious proceeding as being a surprise not unattended by some degree of negligence; nor do I doubt that if any such act of violence had been apprehended thousands of the good citizens of Boston would have presented themselves voluntarily and promptly to prevent it. But the danger does not seem to have been timely made known or duly appreciated by those who were concerned in the execution of the process. In a community distinguished for its love of order and respect for the laws, among a people whose sentiment is liberty and law, and not liberty without law nor above the law, such an outrage could only be the

---

*James D. Richardson, ed. *The Messages and Papers of the Presidents.* Vol. 6, New York, 1897, p. 2637.

result of sudden violence, unhappily too much unprepared for to be successfully resisted. It would be melancholy indeed if we were obliged to regard this outbreak against the constitutional and legal authority of the Government as proceeding from the general feeling of the people in a spot which is proverbially called "the Cradle of American Liberty," Such, undoubtedly, is not the fact. It violates without question the general sentiment of the people of Boston and of a vast majority of the whole people of Massachusetts, as much as it violates the law, defies the authority of the Government, and disgraces those concerned in it, their aiders and abettors.

RESOLUTION TO AID THE HUNGARIAN REVOLUTIONISTS*
March 3, 1851

This joint congressional resolution is interesting in the light of being an official departure from the principle of non-intervention incorporated in the Monroe Doctrine. Although President Fillmore admired the acts of courage displayed by Louis Kossith's supporters against the Austrian monarchy, he was not disposed to use any action that would cause the United States to become involved in the issue. This resolution irritated the President, and he felt the Thirty-first Congress was catering to public opinion, rather than to the interests of the nation. The President, however, did send a relief ship to Louis Kossuth and his revolutionists, who were on Turkish soil, and enabled them to leave European waters. (See Second Annual message.)

Whereas, the people of the United States sincerely sympathize with the Hungarian exiles, Kossuth and his associates, and fully appreciate the magnanimous conduct of the Turkish government in receiving and treating those noble exiles with kindness and hospitality, and whereas, if it be the wish of these exiles to emigrate to the United States, and the will of the Sultan to permit them to leave his dominions, therefore,

Resolved by the Senate and House of Representatives of the United States of America in Congress assembled, That the President of the United States be, and he hereby is, requested to authorize the employment of some one of the public vessels which may be now cruising in the Meditterranean, to receive and convey to the United States the said Louis Kossuth and his associates in captivity.

Approved, March 3, 1851.

---

*Statutes at Large and Treaties of the United States of America. Vol. 9, Boston, p. 647.

SECOND ANNUAL MESSAGE*
December 2, 1851

The President's second message to Congress is interesting because of the tranquil nature of the address. Weeks prior to this speech, the state elections returns had severely lessened Whig power throughout the nation, and the President had serious doubts for the Party's continuation; he was deeply distressed by this, but his address was controlled and objective.

Toward the closing of his message, the President again called for sectional support of the Compromise of 1850, especially alluding to the Fugitive Slave Act. His words against would-be nullifiers of federal law were leveled at Garrisionian abolitionists as well as southern secessionists.

A movement to amend the Fugitive Slave Act and the popular sovereignty principles of the Utah and New Mexico laws was gaining adherents in both the Whig and "Conscience" Democratic groups. A flat statement against any weakening of the Compromise provisions was included in the President's bid for national unity.

Since the close of the last Congress certain Cubans and other foreigners resident in the United States, who were more or less concerned in the previous invasion of Cuba, instead of being discouraged by its failure have again abused the hospitality of this country by making it the scene of the equipment of another military expedition against that possession of Her Catholic Majesty, in which they were countenanced, aided, and joined by citizens of the United States. On receiving intelligence that such designs were entertained, I lost no time in issuing such instructions to the proper officers of the United States as seemed to be called for by the occasion. By the proclamation a copy of which is herewith submitted I also warned those who might be in danger of being inveigled into this scheme of its unlawful character and of the penalties which they would incur. For some time there was reason to hope, however, proved to be delusive. Very early in the morning of the 3d of August a steamer called the Pampero departed from New Orleans for Cuba, having on board upward of 400 armed men with evident intentions to make war upon the authorities of the island. This expedition was set on foot in palpable violation of the laws of the United States. Its leader was a Spaniard, and several of the chief officers and some others engaged in it were foreigners. The persons composing it, however, were mostly citizens of the United States.

---

*James D. Richardson, ed. *The Messages and Papers of the Presidents.* Vol. 6, New York, pp. 2651–2666.

Before the expedition set out, and probably before it was organized, a slight insurrectionary movement, which appears to have been soon suppressed, had taken place in the eastern quarter of Cuba. The importance of this movement was, unfortunately, so much exaggerated in the accounts of it published in this country that these adventurers seem to have been led to believe that the Creole population of the island not only desired to throw off the authority of the mother country, but had resolved upon that step and had begun a well-concerted enterprise for effecting it. The persons engaged in the expedition were generally young and ill informed. The steamer in which they embarked left New Orleans stealthily and without a clearance. After touching at Key West, she proceeded to the coast of Cuba, and on the night between the 11th and 12th of August landed the persons on board at Playtas, within about 20 leagues of Havana.

The main body of them proceeded to and took possession of an inland village 6 leagues distant, leaving other to follow in charge of the baggage as soon as the means of transportation could be obtained. The latter, having taken up their line of march to connect themselves with the main body, and having proceeded about 4 leagues into the country, were attacked on the morning of the 13th by a body of Spanish troops, and a bloody conflict ensued, after which they retreated to the place of disembarkation, where about 50 of them obtained boats and reembarked therein. They were, however, intercepted among the keys near the shore by a Spanish steamer cruising on the coast, captured and carried to Havana, and after being examined before a military court were sentenced to be publicly executed, and the sentence was carried into effect on the 16th of August.

On receiving information of what had occurred Commodore Foxhill A. Parker was instructed to proceed in the steam frigate Saranac to Havana and inquire into the charges against the persons executed, the circumstances under which they were taken, and whatsoever referred to their trial and sentence. Copies of the instructions from the Department of State to him and of his letters to that Department are herewith submitted.

According to the record of the examination, the prisoners all admitted the offenses charged against them, of being hostile invaders of the island. At the time of their trial and execution the main body of the invaders was still in the field making war upon the Spanish authorities and Spanish subjects. After the lapse of some days, being overcome by the Spanish troops, they dispersed on the 24th of August. Lopez, their leader, was captured some days after, and executed on the 1st of September. Many of his remaining followers were killed or died of hunger and fatigue, and the rest were made prisoners. Of these none appear to have been tried or executed. Several of them were pardoned upon application of their friends and others, and the rest, about 160 in number, were sent to Spain. Of the final disposition made of these we have no official information.

Such is the melancholy result of this illegal and ill-fated expedition. Thus thoughtless young men have been induced by false and fraudulent representations to violate the law of their country through rash and unfounded expectations of assisting to accomplish political revolutions in other states, and have lost their lives in the undertaking. Too severe a judgment can hardly be passed by the indignant sense of the community upon those who, being better informed themselves, have yet led away the ardor of youth and an ill-directed love of political liberty. The correspondence between this Government and that of Spain relating to this transaction is herewith communicated.

Although these offenders against the laws have forfeited the protection of their country, yet the Government may, so far as consistent with its obligations to other countries and its fixed purpose to maintain and enforce the laws, entertain sympathy for their unoffending families and friends, as well as a feeling of compassion for themselves. Accordingly, no proper effort has been spared and none will be spared to procure the release of such citizens of the United States engaged in this unlawful enterprise as are now in confinement in Spain; but it is to be hoped that such interposition with the Government of that country may not be considered as affording any ground of expectation that the Government of the United States will hereafter feel itself under any obligation of duty to intercede for the liberation or pardon of such persons as are flagrant offenders against the law of nations and the laws of the United States. These laws must be executed. If we desire to maintain our respectability among the nations of the earth, it behooves us to enforce steadily and sternly the neutrality acts passed by Congress and to follow as far as may be the violation of those acts with condign punishment.

But what gives a peculiar criminality to this invasion of Cuba is that, under the lead of Spanish subjects and with the aid of citizens of the United States, it had its origin with many in motives of cupidity. Money was advanced by individuals, probably in considerable amounts, to purchase Cuban bonds, as they have been called, issued by Lopez, sold, doubtless, at a very large discount, and for the payment of which the public lands and public property of Cuba, of whatever kind, and the fiscal resources of the people and government of that island, from whatever source to be derived, were pledged, as well as the good faith of the government expected to be established. All these means of payment, it is evident, were only to be obtained by a process of bloodshed, war, and revolution. None will deny that those who set on foot military expeditions against foreign states by means like these are far more culpable than the ignorant and the necessitous whom they induce to go forth as the ostensible parties in the proceeding. These originators of the invasion of Cuba seem to have determined with coolness and system upon an undertaking which should disgrace their country, violate its laws, and put to hazard the lives of ill-informed and deluded men. You will consider whether further legislation be necessary to prevent the perpetration of such offenses in future.

No individuals have a right to hazard the peace of the country or to violate its laws upon vague notions of altering or reforming governments in other states. This principle is not only reasonable in itself and in accordance with public law, but is ingrafted into the codes of other nations as well as our own. But while such are the sentiments of this Government, it may be added that every independent nation must be presumed to be able to defend its possessions against unauthorized individuals banded together to attack them. The Government of the United States at all times since its establishment has abstained and has sought to restrain the citizens of the country from entering into controversies between other powers, and to observe all the duties of neutrality. At an early period of the Government, in the Administration of Washington, several laws were passed for this purpose. The main provisions of these laws were reenacted by the act of April, 1818, by which, amongst other things, it was declared that —

> If any person shall, within the territory or jurisdiction of the United States, begin, or set on foot, or provide or prepare the means for, any military expedition or enterprise to be carried on from thence against the territory or domains of any foreign prince or state, or of any colony, district, or people, with whom the United States are at peace, every person so offending shall be deemed guilty of a high misdemeanor, and shall be fined not exceeding $3,000 and imprisoned not more than three years.

And this law has been executed and enforced to the full extent of the power of the Government from that day to this.

In proclaiming and adhering to the doctrine of neutrality and non-intervention, the United States have not followed the lead of other civilized nations; they have taken the lead themselves and have been followed by others. This was admitted by one of the most eminent of modern British statesmen, who said in Parliament, while a minister of the Crown, "that if he wished for a guide in a system of neutrality he should take that laid down by America in the days of Washington and the secretaryship of Jefferson;" and we see, in fact, that the act of Congress of 1818 was followed the succeeding year by an act of the Parliament of England substantially the same in its general provisions. Up to that time there had been no similar law in England, except certain highly penal statutes passed in the reign of George II, prohibiting English subjects from enlisting in foreign service, the avowed object of which statutes was that foreign armies, raised for the purpose of restoring the house of Stuart to the throne, should not be strengthened by recruits from England herself.

All must see that difficulties may arise in carrying the laws referred to into execution in a country now having 3,000 or 4,000 miles of seacoast, with an infinite number of ports and harbors and small inlets, from some of which unlawful expeditions may suddenly set forth, without the knowledge of Government, against the possessions of foreign states.

"Friendly relations with all, but entangling alliances with none," has long been a maxim with us. Our true mission is not to propagate our opinions or impose upon other countries our form of government by artifice or force, but to teach by example and show by our success, moderation, and justice the blessings of self-government and the advantages of free institutions. Let every people choose for itself and make and alter its political institutions to suit its own condition and convenience. But while we avow and maintain this neutral policy ourselves, we are anxious to see the same forbearance on the part of other nations whose forms of government are different from our own. The deep interest which we feel in the spread of liberal principles and the establishment of free governments and the sympathy with which we witness every struggle against oppression forbid that we should be indifferent to a case in which the strong arm of a foreign power is invoked to stifle public sentiment and repress the spirit of freedom in any country.

The Turkish Government has expressed its thanks for the kind reception given to the Sultan's agent, Amin Bey, on the occasion of his recent visit to the United States. On the 28th of February last a dispatch was addressed by the Secretary of State to Mr. Marsh, the American minister at Constantinople, instructing him to ask of the Turkish Government permission for the Hungarians then imprisoned within the dominions of the Sublime Porte to remove to this country. On the 3d of March last both Houses of Congress passed a resolution requesting the President to authorize the employment of a public vessel to convey to this country Louis Kossuth and his associates in captivity.

The instruction above referred to was complied with, and the Turkish Government having released Governor Kossuth and his companions from prison, on the 10th of September last they embarked on board of the United States steam frigate Mississippi, which was selected to carry into effect the resolution of Congress. Governor Kossuth left the Mississippi at Gibraltar for the purpose of making a visit to England, and may shortly be expected in New York. By communications to the Department of State he has expressed his grateful acknowledgments for the interposition of this Government in behalf of himself and his associates. This country has been justly regarded as a safe asylum for those whom political events have exiled from their own homes in Europe, and it is recommended to Congress to consider in what manner Governor Kossuth and his companions, brought hither by its authority, shall be received and treated. . . .

The production of gold in California for the past year seems to promise a large supply of that metal from that quarter for some time to come. This large annual increase of the currency of the world must be attended with its usual results. These have been already partially disclosed in the enhancement of prices and a rising spirit of speculation and adventure, tending to overtrading, as well at home as abroad. Unless some salutary check shall be given to these tendencies it is to be feared that importations of foreign goods beyond a healthy demand in this country will lead to a sudden drain of the precious metals from us, bringing with it, as it has done in former times, the most disastrous consequences to the business and capital of the American people.

The exports of specie to liquidate our foreign debt during the past fiscal year have been $24,263,979 over the amount of specie imported. The exports of specie during the first quarter of the present fiscal year have been $14,651,827. Should specie continue to be exported at this rate for the remaining three quarters of this year, it will drain from our metallic currency during the year ending 30th June, 1852, the enormous amount of $58,607,308.

In the present prosperous condition of the national finances it will become the duty of Congress to consider the best mode of paying off the public debt. If the present and anticipated surplus in the Treasury should not be absorbed by appropriations of an extraordinary character, this surplus should be employed in such way and under such restrictions as Congress may enact in extinguishing the outstanding debt of the nation.

By reference to the act of Congress approved 9th September, 1850, it will be seen that, in consideration of certain concessions by the State of Texas, it is provided that —

> The United States shall pay to the State of Texas the sum of $10,000,000 in a stock bearing 5 per cent interest and redeemable at the end of fourteen years, the interest payable half-yearly at the Treasury of the United States.

In the same section of the law it is further provided —

> That no more than five millions of said stock shall be issued until the creditors of the State holding bonds and other certificates of stock of Texas, for which duties on imports were specially pledged, shall first file at the Treasury of the United States releases of all claims against the United States for or on account of said bonds or certificates, in such form as shall be prescribed by the Secretary of the Treasury and approved by the President of the United States.

The form of release thus provided for has been prescribed by the Secretary of the Treasury and approved. It has been published in all the leading newspapers in the commercial cities of the United States, and all persons holding claims of the kind specified in the foregoing provison were required to file their releases (in the form thus prescribed in the Treasury of the United States on or before the 1st day of October, 1851. Although this publication has been continued from the 25th day of March, 1851, yet up to the 1st of October last comparatively few releases had been filed by the creditors of Texas.

The authorities of the State of Texas, at the request of the Secretary of the Treasury, have furnished a schedule of the public debt of that State created prior to her admission into the Union, with a copy of the laws under which each class was contracted.

In my last annual message, to which I respectfully refer, I stated briefly the reasons which induced me to recommend a modification of the present tariff by converting the ad valorem into a specific duty wherever the article imported was of such a character as to permit it, and that such a discrimination should be made in favor of the industrial pursuits of our own country as to encourage home production without excluding foreign competition.

The numerous frauds which continue to be practiced upon the revenue by false invoices and undervaluations constitute an unanswerable reason for adopting specific instead of ad valorem duties in all cases where the nature of the commodity does not forbid it. A striking illustration of these frauds will be exhibited in the report of the Secretary of the Treasury, showing the custom-house valuation of articles imported under a former law, subject to specific duties, when there was no inducement to undervaluation, and the custom-house valuations of the same articles under the present system of ad valorem duties, so greatly reduced as to leave no doubt of the existence of the most flagrant abuses under the existing laws. This practical evasion of the present law, combined with the languishing condition of some of the great interests of the country, caused by overimportations and consequent depressed prices, and with the failure in obtaining a foreign market for our increasing surplus of breadstuffs and provisions, has induced me again to recommend a modification of the existing tariff.

The report of the Secretary of the Interior, which accompanies this communication, will present a condensed statement of the operations of that important Department of the Government.

It will be seen that the cash sales of the public lands exceed those of the preceeding year, and that there is reason to anticipate a still further increase, notwithstanding the large donations which have been made to many of the States and the liberal grants to individuals as a reward for military services. This fact furnishes very gratifying evidence of the growing wealth and prosperity of our country.

The large accessions to our Indian population consequent upon the acquisition of New Mexico and California and the extension of our settlements into Utah and Oregon have given increased interest and importance to our relations with the aboriginal race.

No material change has taken place within the last year in the condition and prospects of the Indian tribes who reside in the Northwestern Territory and west of the Mississippi River. We are at peace with all of them, and it will be a source of pleasure to you to learn that they are gradually advancing in civilization and the pursuits of social life.

Along the Mexican frontier and in California and Oregon there have been occasional manifestations of unfriendly feeling and some depredations committed. I am satisfied, however, that they resulted more from the destitute and starving condition of the Indians than from any settled hostility toward the whites. As the settlements of our citizens progress toward them, the game, upon which they mainly rely for subsistence, is driven off or destroyed, and the only alternative left to them is starvaion or plunder. It becomes us to consider, in view of this condition of things, whether justice and humanity, as well as an enlightened economy, do not require that instead of seeking to punish them for offenses which are the result of our own policy toward them we should not provide for their immediate wants and encourage them to engage in agriculture and to rely on their labor instead of the chase for the means of support.

Various important treaties have been negotiated with different tribes during the year, by which their title to large and valuable tracts of country has been extinguished, all of which will at the proper time be submitted to the Senate for ratification.

In my last annual message I gave briefly my reasons for believing that you possessed the constitutional power to improve the harbors of our Great Lakes and seacoast and the navigation of our principal rivers, and recommended that appropriations should be made for completing such works as had already been commenced and for commencing such others as might seem to the wisdom of Congress to be of public and general importance. Without repeating the reasons then urged, I deem it my duty again to call your attention to this important subject. The works on many of the harbors were left in an unfinished state, and consequently exposed to the action of the elements, which is fast destroying them. Great numbers of lives and vast amounts of property are annually lost for want of safe and convenient harbors on the Lakes. None but those who have been exposed to that dangerous navigation can fully appreciate the importance of this subject. The whole Northwest appeals to you for relief, and I trust their appeal will receive due consideration at your hands.

The same is in a measure true in regard to some of the harbors and inlets on the seacoast.

The unobstructed navigation of our large rivers is of equal importance. Our settlements are now extending to the sources of the great rivers which empty into and form a part of the Mississippi, and the value of the public lands in those regions would be greatly enhanced by freeing the navigation of those waters from obstructions. In view, therefore, of this great interest, I deem it my duty again to urge upon Congress to make such appropriations for these improvements as they may deem necessary.

The public statutes of the United States have now been accumulating for more than sixty years, and, interspersed with private acts, are scattered through numerous volumes, and, from the cost of the whole, have become almost inaccessible to the great mass of the community. They also exhibit much of the incongruity and imperfection of hasty legislation. As it seems to be generally conceded that there is no "common law" of the United States to supply the defects of their legislation, it is most important that that legislation should be as perfect as possible, defining every power intended to be conferred, every crime intended to be made punishable, and prescribing the punishment to be inflicted. In addition to some particular cases spoken of more at length, the whole criminal code is now lamentably defective. Some offenses are imperfectly described and others are entirely omitted, so that flagrant crimes may be committed with impunity. The scale of punishment is not in all cases graduated according to the degree and nature of the offense, and is often rendered more unequal by the different modes of imprisonment or penitentiary confinement in the different States.

Many laws of a permanent character have been introduced into appropriation bills, and it is often difficult to determine whether the particular clause expires with the temporary act of which it is a part or continues in force. It has also frequently happened that enactments and provisions of law have been introduced into bills with the title or general subject of which they have little or no connection or relation. In this mode of legislation so many enactments have been heaped upon each other, and often with but little consideration, that in many instances it is difficult to search out and determine what is the law.

The Government of the United States is emphatically a government of written laws. The statutes should therefore, as far as practicable, not only be made accessible to all, but be expressed in language so plain and simple as to be understood by all and arranged in such method as to give perspicuity to every subject. Many of the States have revised their public acts with great and manifest benefit, and I recommend that provision be made by law for the appointment of a commission to revise the public statutes of the United States, arranging them in order, supplying deficiencies, correcting incongruities, simplifying their language, and reporting them to Congress for its action. . . .

It is deeply to be regretted that in several instances officers of the Government, in attempting to execute the law for the return of fugitives from labor, have been openly resisted and their efforts frustrated and defeated by lawless and violent mobs; that in one case such resistance resulted in the death of an estimable citizen, and in others serious injury ensued to those officers and to individuals who were using their endeavors to sustain the laws. Prosecutions have been instituted against the alleged offenders so far as they could be identified, and are still pending. I have regarded it as my duty in these cases to give all aid legally in my power to the enforcement of the laws, and I shall continue to do so wherever and whenever their execution may be resisted.

The act of Congress for the return of fugitives from labor is one required and demanded by the express words of the Constitution.

The Constitution declares that —

> No person held to service or labor in one State, under the laws thereof, escaping into another, shall, in consequence of any law or regulation therein, be discharged from such service or labor, but shall be delivered up on claim of the party to whom such service or labor may be due.

This constitutional provision is equally obligatory upon the legislative, the executive, and judicial departments of the Government, and upon every citizen of the United States.

Congress, however, must from necessity first act act upon the subject by prescribing the proceedings necessary to ascertain that the person is a fugitive and the means to be used for his restoration to the claimant. This was done by an act passed during the first term of President Washington, which was amended by that enacted by the last Congress, and it now remains for the executive and judicial departments to take care that these laws be faithfully executed. This injunction of the Constitution is as peremptory and as binding as any other; it stands exactly on the same foundation as that clause which provides for the return of fugitives from justice, or that which declares that no bill of attainder or ex post facto law shall be passed, or that which provides for an equality of taxation according to the census, or the clause declaring that all duties shall be uniform throughout the United States, or the important provision that the trial of all crimes shall be by jury. the same authority, must stand or fall together. Some objections have been urged against the details of the act for the return of fugitives from labor, but it is worthy of remark that the main opposition is aimed against the Constitution intself, and proceeds from persons and classes of persons many of whom declare their wish to see that Constitution overturned. They avow their hostility to any law which shall give full and practical effect to this requirement of the Constitution. Fortunately, the number of these persons is comparatively small, and is believed to be daily diminishing; but the issue which they present is one which involves the supremacy and even the existence of the Constitution.

Cases have heretofore arisen in which individuals have denied the binding authority of acts of Congress, and even States have proposed to nullify such acts upon the ground that the Constitution was the supreme law of the land, and that those acts of Congress were repugnant to that instrument; but nullification is now aimed not so much against particular laws as being inconsistent with the Constitution as against the Constitution itself, and it is not to be disguised that a spirit exists, and has been actively at work, to rend asunder this Union, which is our cherished inheritance from our Revolutionary fathers.

In my last annual message I stated that I considered the series of measures which had been adopted at the previous session in reference to the agitation growing out of the Territorial and slavery questions as a final settlement in principle and substance of the dangerous and exciting subjects which they embraced, and I recommended adherence to the adjustment established by those measures until time and experience should demonstrate the necessity of further legislation to guard against evasion or abuse. I was not induced to make this recommendation because I thought those measures perfect, for no human legislation can be perfect. Wide differences and jarring opinions can only be reconciled by yielding something on all sides, and this result had been reached after an angry conflict of many months, in which one part of the country was arrayed against another, and violent convulsion seemed to be imminent. Looking at the interests of the whole country, I felt it to be my duty to seize upon this compromise as the best that could be obtained amid conflicting interests and to insist upon it as a final settlement, to be adhered to by all who value the peace and welfare of the country. A year has now elapsed since that recommendation was made. To that recommendation I still adhere, and I congratulate you and the country upon the general acquiescence in these measures of peace which has been exhibited in all parts of the Republic. And not only is there this general acquiescence in these measures, but the spirit of conciliation which has been manifested in regard to them in all parts of the country has removed doubts and uncertainties in the minds of thousands of good men concerning the durability of our popular institutions and given renewed assurance that our liberty and our Union may subsist together for the benefit of this and all succeeding generations.

THIRD ANNUAL MESSAGE*
December 6, 1852

President Fillmore, now an interregnum executive, elaborated on the blessings and strengths of the United States. He began his message with a eulogy to Daniel Webster, the very image of union, and closed with a statement of liberty under the Constitution. No mention is made of the sectional strife that had become inflamed during his term in office, and a moment of respite for the nation appeared to have been reached. A statement to continue the traditional non-involvement principles of the Monroe Doctrine is re[p]eated again by Fillmore, and the sections dealing with the American Indian tribes in the West is enlightening for the reader.

Fellow-Citizens of the Senate and of the House of Representatives:

The brief space which has elapsed since the close of your last session has been marked by no extraordinary political event. The quadrennial election of Chief Magistrate has passed off with less than the usual excitement. However individuals and parties may have been disappointed in the result, it is, nevertheless, a subject of national congratulation that the choice has been effected by the independent suffrages of a free people, undisturbed by those influences which in other countries have too often affected the purity of popular elections.

Our grateful thanks are due to an all-merciful Providence, not only for staying the pestilence which in different forms has desolated some of our cities, but for crowning the labors of the husbandman with an abundant harvest and the nation generally with the blessings of peace and prosperity.

Within a few weeks the public mind has been deeply affected by the death of Daniel Webster, filling at his decease the office of Secretary of State. His associates in the executive government have sincerely sympathized with his family and the public generally on this mournful occasion. His commanding talents, his great political and professional eminence, his well-tried patriotism, and his long and faithful services in the most important public trusts have caused his dath to be lamented throughout the country and have earned for him a lasting place in our history.

---

*James D. Richardson, ed. *The Messages and Papers of the Presidents.* Vol. 6, New York, 1897, pp. 2673–*2688.*

The affairs of Cuba formed a prominent topic in my last annual message. They remain in an uneasy condition, and a feeling of alarm and irritation on the part of the Cuban authorities appears to exist. This feeling has interfered with the regular commercial intercourse between the United States and the island and led to some acts of which we have a right to complain. But the Captain-General of Cuba is clothed with no power to treat with foreign governments, nor is he in any degree under the control of the Spanish minister at Washington. Any communication which he may hold with an agent of a foreign power is informal and matter of courtesy. Anxious to put an end to the existing inconveniences (which seemed to rest on a misconception), I directed the newly appointed minister to Mexico to visit Havana on his way to Vera Cruz. He was respectfully received by the Captain-General, who conferred with him freely on the recent occurrences, but no permanent arrangement was affected.

In the meantime the refusal of the Captain-General to allow passengers and the mail to be landed in certain cases, for a reason which does not furnish, in the opinion of this Government, even a good presumptive ground for such prohibition, has been made the subject of a serious remonstrance at Madrid, and I have no reason to doubt that due respect will be paid by the Government of Her Catholic Majesty to the representations which our minister has been instructed to make on the subject.

It is but justice to the Captain-General to add that his conduct toward the steamers employed to carry the mails of the United States to Havana has, with the exceptions above alluded to, been marked with kindness and liberality, and indicates no general purpose of interfering with the commercial correspondence and intercourse between the island and this country.

Early in the present year official notes were received from the ministers of France and England inviting the Government of the United States to become a party with Great Britain and France to a tripartite convention, in virtue of which the three powers should severally and collectively disclaim now and for the future all intention to obtain possession of the island of Cuba, and should bind themselves to discountenance all attempts to that effect on the part of any power or individual whatever. This invitation has been respectfully declined, for reasons which it would occupy too much space in this communication to state in detail, but which led me to think that the proposed measure would be of doubtful constitutionality, impolitic, and unavailing. I have, however, in common with several of my predecessors, directed the ministers of France and England to be assured that the United States entertain no designs against Cuba, but that, on the contrary, I should regard its incorporation into the Union at the present time as fraught with serious peril.

Were this island comparatively destitute of inhabitants or occupied by a kindred race, I should regard it, if voluntarily ceded by Spain, as a most desirable acquisition. But under existing circumstances I should look upon its incorporation into our Union as a very hazardous measure. It would bring into the Confederacy a population of a different national stock, speaking a different language, and not likely to harmonize with the other members. It would probably affect in a prejudicial manner the industrial interests of the South, and it might revive those conflicts of opinion between the different sections of the country which lately shook the Union to its center, and which have been so happily compromised. . . .

Our settlements on the shores of the Pacific have already given a great extension, and in some respects a new direction, to our commerce in that ocean. A direct and rapidly increasing intercourse has sprung up with eastern Asia. The waters of the Northern Pacific, even into the Arctic Sea, have of late years been frequented by our whalemen. The application of steam to the general purposes of navigation is becoming daily more common, and makes it desirable to obtain fuel and other necessary supplies at convenient points on the route between Asia and our Pacific shores. Our unfortunate countrymen who from tim to time suffer shipwreck on the coasts of the eastern seas are entitled to protection. Besides these specific objects, the general prosperity of our States on the Pacific requires that an attempt should be made to open the opposite regions of Asia to a mutually beneficial intercourse. It is obvious that this attempt could be made by no power to so great advantage as by the United States, whose constitutional system excludes every idea of distant colonial dependencies. I have accordingly been led to order an appropriate naval force to Japan, under the command of a discreet and intelligent officer of the highest rank known to our service. He is instructed to endeavor to obtain from the Government of that country some relaxation of the inhospitable and antisocial system which it has pursued for about two centuries. He has been directed particularly to remonstrate in the strongest language against the cruel treatment to which our shipwrecked mariners have often been subjected and to insist that they shall be treated with humanity. He is instructed, however, at the same time, to give that Government the amplest assurances that the objects of the United States are such, and such only, as I have indicated, and that the expedition is friendly and peaceful. Notwithstanding the jealousy with which the Governments of eastern Asia regard all overtures from foreigners, I am not without hopes of a beneficial result of the expedition. Should it be crowned with success, the advantages will not be confined to the United States, but, as in the case of China, will be equally enjoyed by all the other maritime powers. I have much satisfaction in stating that in all the steps preparatory to this expedition the Government of the United States has been materially aided by the good offices of the King of the Netherlands, the only European power having any commerical relations with Japan.

In my first annual message to Congress I called your attention to what seemed to me some defects in the present tariff, and recommended such modifications as in my judgment were best adapted to remedy its evils and promote the prosperity of the country. Nothing has since occurred to change my views on this important question.

Without repeating the arguments contained in my former message in favor of discriminating protective duties, I deem it my duty to call your attention to one or two other considerations affecting this subject. The first is the effect of large importations of foreign goods upon our currency. Most of the gold of California, as fast as it is coined, finds its way directly to Europe in payment for goods purchased. In the second place, as our manufacturing establishments are broken down by competition with foreigners, the capital invested in them is lost, thousands of honest and industrious citizens are thrown out of employment, and the farmer, to that extent, is deprived of a home market for the sale of his surplus produce. In the third place, the destruction of our manufactures leaves the foreigner without competition in our market, and he consequently raises the price of the article sent here for sale, as is now seen in the increased cost of iron imported from England. The prosperity and wealth of every nation must depend upon its productive industry. The farmer is stimulated to exertion by finding a ready market for his surplus products, and benefited by being able to exchange them without loss of time or expense of transportation for the manufactures which his comfort or convenience requires. This is always done to the best advantage where a portion of the community in which he lives is engaged in other pursuits. But most manufactures require an amount of capital and a practical skill which can not be commanded unless they be protected for a time from ruinous competiton from abroad. Hence the necessity of laying those duties upon imported goods which the Constitution authorizes for revenue in such a manner as to protect and encourage the labor of our own citizens. Duties, however, should not be fixed at a rate so high as to exclude the foreign aritcle, but should be so graduated as to enable the domestic manufacturer fairly to compete with the foreigner in our own markets, and by this competition to reduce the price of the manufactured article to the consumer to the lowest rate at which it can be produced. This policy would place the mechanic by the side of the farmer, create a mutual interchange of their respective commodities, and thus stimulate the industry of the whole country and render us independent of foreign nations for the supplies required by the habits or necessities of the people.

Another question, wholly independent of protection, presents itself, and that is, whether the duties levied should be upon the value of the article at the place of shipment, or, where it is practicable, a specific duty, graduated according to qunatity, as ascertained by weight or measure. All our duties are at present ad valorem. A certain percentage is levied on the price of the goods at the port of shipment in a foreign country. Most commercial nations have found it indispensable, for the purpose of preventing fraud and perjury, to make the duties specific whenever the article is of such a uniform value in weight or measure as to justify such a duty. Legislation should never encourage dishonesty or crime. It is impossible that the revenue officers at the port where the goods are entered and the duties paid should know with certainty what they cost in the foreign country. Yet the law requires that they should levy the duty according to such cost. They are therefore compelled to resort to very unsatisfactory evidence to ascertain what that cost was. They take the invoice of the importer, attested by his oath, as the best evidence of which the nature of the case admits. But everyone must see that the invoice may be fabricated and the oath by which it is supported false, by reason of which the dishonest importer pays a part only of the duties which are paid by the honest one, and thus indirectly receives from the Treasury of the United States a reward for his fraud and perjury. The reports of the Secretary of the Treasury heretofore made on this subject show conclusively that these frauds have been practiced to a great extent. The tendency is to destroy that high moral character for which our merchants have long been distinguished, to defraud the Government of its revenue, to break down the honest importer by a dishonest competition, and, finally, to transfer the business of importation to foreign and irresponsible agents, to the great detriment of our citizens. I therefore again most earnestly recommend the adoption of specific duties wherever it is practicable, or a home valuation, to prevent these frauds.

I would also again call your attention to the fact that the present tariff in some cases imposes a higher duty upon the raw material imported than upon the article manufactured from it, the consequence of which is that the duty operates to the encouragement of the foreigner and the discouragement of our own citizens.

The Senate not having thought proper to ratify the treaties which have been negotiated with the tribes of Indians in California and Oregon, our relations with them have been left in a very unsatisfactory condition.

In other parts of our territory particular districts of country have been set apart for the exclusive occupation of the Indians, and their right to the lands within those limits has been acknowledged and respected. But in California and Oregon there has been no recognition by the Government of the exclusive right of the Indians to any part of the country. They are therefore mere tenants at sufferance, and liable to be driven from place to place at the pleasure of the whites.

The treaties which have been rejected proposed to remedy this evil by allotting to the different tribes districts of country suitable to their habits of life and sufficient for their support. This provision, more than any other, it is believed, led to their rejection; and as no substitute for it has been adopted by Congress, it has not been deemed advisable to attempt to enter into new treaties of a permanent character, although no effort has been spared by temporary arrangements to preserve friendly relations with them.

If it be the desire of Congress to remove them from the country altogether, or to assign to them particular districts more remote from the settlements of the whites, it will be proper to set apart by law the territory which they are to occupy and to provide the means necessary for removing them to it. Justice alike to our own citizens and to the Indians requires the prompt action of Congress on this subject.

The amendments proposed by the Senate to the treaties which were negotiated with the Sioux Indians of Minnesota have been submitted to the tribes who were parties to them, and have received their assent. A large tract of valuable territory has thus been opened for settlement and cultivation, and all danger of collision with these powerful and warlike bands has been happily removed.

The removal of the remnant of the tribe of Seminole Indians from Florida has long been a cherished object of the Government, and it is one to which my attention has been steadily directed. Admonished by past experience of the difficulty and cost of the attempt to remove them by military force, resort has been had to conciliatory measures. By the invitation of the Commissioner of Indian Affairs, several of the principal chiefs recently visited Washington, and whilst here acknowledged in writing the obligation of their tribe to remove with the least possible delay. Late advices from the special agent of the Government represent that they adhere to their promise, and that a council of their people has been called to make their preliminary arrangements. A general emigration may therefore be confidently expected at an early day.

Every effort has been made to protect our frontier and that of the adjoining Mexican States from the incursions of the Indian tribes. Of about 11,000 men of which the Army is composed, nearly 8,000 are employed in the defense of the newly acquired territory (including Texas) and of emigrants proceeding thereto. I am gratified to say that these efforts have been unusually successful. With the exception of some partial outbreaks in California and Oregon and occasional depredations on a portion of the Rio Grande, owing, it is believed, to the disturbed state of that border region, the inroads of the Indians have been effectually restrained.

Experience has shown, however, that whenever the two races are brought into contact collisions will inevitably occur. To prevent these collisions the United States have generally set apart portions of their territory for the exclusive occupation of the Indian tribes. A difficulty occurs, however, in the application of this policy to Texas. By the terms of the compact by which that State was admitted into the Union she retained the ownership of all the vacant lands within her limits.

The government of that State, it is understood, has assigned no portion of her territory to the Indians, but as fast as her settlements advance lays it off into counties and proceeds to survey and sell it. This policy manifestly tends not only to alarm and irritate the Indians, but to compel them to resort to plunder for subsistence. It also deprives this Government of that influence and control over them without which no durable peace can ever exist between them and the whites. I trust, therefore, that a due regard for her own interests, apart from considerations of humanity and justice, will induce that State to assign a small portion of her vast domain for the provisional occupancy of the small remnants of tribes within her borders, subject, of course, to her ownership and eventual jurisdiction. If she should fail to do this, the fulfillment of our treaty stipulations with Mexico and our duty to the Indians themselves will, it is feared, become a subject of serious embarrassment to the Government. It is hoped, however, that a timely and just provision by Texas may avert this evil.

I think it due to the several Executive Departments of this Government to bear testimony to the efficiency and integrity with which they are conducted. With all the careful superintendence which it is possible for the heads of those Departments to exercise, still the due administration and guardianship of the public money must very much depend on the vigilance, intelligence, and fidelity of the subordinate officers and clerks, and especially on those intrusted with the settlement and adjustment of claims and accounts. I am gratified to believe that they have generally performed their duties faithfully and well. They are appointed to guard the approaches to the public Treasury, and they occupy positions that expose them to all the temptations and seductions which the cupidity of peculators and fraudulent claimants can prompt them to employ. It will be but a wise precaution to protect the Government against that source of mischief and corruption, as far as it can be done, by the enactment of all proper legal penalties. The laws in this respect are supposed to be defective, and I therefore deem it my duty to call your attention to the subject and to recommend that provision be made by law for the punishment not only of those who shall accept bribes, but also of those who shall either promise, give, or offer to give to any of those officers or clerks a bribe or reward touching or relating to any matter of their official action or duty.

It has been the uniform policy of this Government, from its foundation to the present day, to abstain from all interference in the domestic affairs of other nations. The consequence has been that while the nations of Europe have been engaged in desolating wars our country has pursued its peaceful course to unexampled prosperity and happiness. The wars in which we have been compelled to engage in defense of the rights and honor of the country have been, fortunately, of short duration. During the terrific contest of nation against nation which succeeded the French Revolution we were enabled by the wisdom and firmness of President Washington to maintain our neutrality.

While other nations were drawn into this wide-sweeping whirlpool, we sat quiet and unmoved upon our own shores. While the flower of their numerous armies was wasted by disease or perished by hundreds of thousands upon the battlefield, the youth of this favored land were permitted to enjoy the blessings of peace beneath the paternal roof. While the States of Europe incurred enormous debts, under the burden of which their subjects still groan, and which must absorb no small part of the product of the honest industry of those countries for generations to come, the United States have once been enabled to exhibit the proud spectacle of a nation free from public debt, and if permitted to pursue our prosperous way for a few years longer in peace we may do the same again.

But it is now said by some that this policy must be changed. Europe is no longer separated from us by a voyage of months, but steam navigation has brought her within a few days sail of our shores. We see more of her movements and take a deeper interest in her controversies. Although no one proposes that we should join the fraternity of potentates who have for ages lavished the blood and treasure of their subjects in maintaining "the balance of power," yet it is said that we ought to interfere between contending sovereigns and their subjects for the purpose of overthrowing the monarchies of Europe and establishing in their place republican institutions. It is alleged that we have heretofore pursued a different course from a sense of our weakness, but that now our conscious strength dictates a change of policy, and that it is consequently our duty to mingle in these contests and aid those who are struggling for liberty.

This is a most seductive but dangerous appeal to the generous sympathies of freemen. Enjoying, as we do, the blessings of a free Government, there is no man who has an American heart that would not rejoice to see these blessings extended to all other nations. We can not witness the struggle between the oppressed and his oppressor anywhere without the deepest sympathy for the former and the most anxious desire for his triumph. Nevertheless, is it prudent or is it wise to involve ourselves in these foreign wars? Is it indeed true that we have heretofore refrained from doing so merely from the degrading motive of a conscious weakness? For the honor of the patriots who have gone before us, I can not admit it. Men of the Revolution, who drew the sword against the oppressions of the mother country and pledged to Heaven "their lives, their fortunes, and their sacred honor" to maintain their freedom, could never have been actuated by so unworthy a motive. They knew no weakness or fear where right or duty pointed the way, and it is a libel upon their fair fame for us, while we enjoy the blessings for which they so nobly fought and bled, to insinuate it. The truth is that the course which they pursued was dictated by a stern sense of international justice, by a statesmanlike prudence and a far-seeing wisdom, looking not merely to the present necessities but to the permanent safety and interest of the country. They knew that the world is governed less by sympathy than by reason and force; that it was not possible for this nation to become a "propagandist" of free principles without arraying against it the combined powers of Europe, and that the result was more likely to be the overthrow of republican liberty here than its establishment there. History has been written in vain for those who can doubt this. France had no sooner established a republican form of government than she manifested a desire to force its blessings on all the world. Her own historian informs us that, hearing of some petty acts of tyranny in a neighboring principality. "the National Convention declared that she would afford succor and fraternity to all nations who wished to recover their liberty, and she gave it in charge to the executive power to give orders to the generals of the French armies to aid all citizens who might have been or should be oppressed in the cause of liberty." Here was the false step which led to her subsequent misfortunes. She soon found herself involved in war with all the rest of Europe. In less than ten years her Government was changed from a republic to an empire, and finally, after shedding rivers of blood, foreign powers restored her exiled dynasty and exhausted Europe sought peace and repose in the unquestioned ascendency of monarchical principles. Let us learn wisdom from her example. Let us remember that revolutions do not always establish freedom. Our own free institutions were not the offspring of our Revolution. They existed before. They were planted in the free charters of self-government under which the English colonies grew up, and our Revolution only freed us from the dominion of a foreign power whose government was at variance with those institutions. But European nations have had no such training for self-government, and every effort to establish it by bloody revolutions has been, and must without that preparation continue to be, a failure, Liberty unregulated by law degenerates into anarchy, which soon becomes the most horrid of all despotisms. Our policy is wisely to govern ourselves, and thereby to set such an example of national justice, prosperity, and true glory as shall teach to all nations the blessings of self-government and the unparalleled enterprise and success of a free people.

We live in an age of progress, and ours is emphatically a country of progress. Within the last half century the number of States in this Union has nearly doubled, the population has almost quadrupled, and our boundaries have been extended from the Mississippi to the Pacific. Our territory is checkered over with railroads and furrowed with canals. The inventive talent of our country is excited to the highest pitch, and the numerous applications for patents for valuable improvements distinguish this age and this people from all others. The genius of one American has enabled our commerce to move against wind and tide and that of another has annihilated distance in the transmission of intelligence. The whole country is full of enterprise. Our common schools are diffusing intelligence among the people and our industry is fast accumulating the comforts and luxuries of life. This is in part owing to our peculiar position, to our fertile soil and comparatively sparse population; but much of it is also owing to the popular institutions under which we live, to the freedom which every man feels to engage in any useful pursuit according to his taste or inclination, and to the entire confidence that his person and property will be protected by the laws. But whatever may be the cause of this unparalleled growth in population, intelligence, and wealth, one thing is clear—that the Government must keep pace with the progress of the people. It must participate in their spirit of enterprise, and while it exacts obedience to the laws and restrains all unauthorized invasions of the rights of neighboring states, it should foster and protect home industry and lend its powerful strength to the improvement of such means of intercommunication as are necessary to promote our internal commerce and strengthen the ties which bind us together as a people.

It is not strange, however much it may be regretted, that such an exuberance of enterprise should cause some individuals to mistake change for progress and the invasion of the rights of others for national prowess and glory. The former are constantly agitating for some change in the organic law, or urging new and untried theories of human rights. The latter are ever ready to engage in any wild crusade against a neighboring people, regardless of the justice of the enterprise and without looking at the fatal consequences to ourselves and to the cause of popular government. Such expeditions, however, are often stimulated by mercenary individuals, who expect to share the plunder or profit of the enterprise without exposing themselves to danger, and are led on by some irresponsible foreigner, who abuses the hospitality of our own Government by seducing the young and ignorant to join in his scheme of personal ambition or revenge under the false and delusive pretense of extending the area of freedom. These reprehensible aggressions but retard the true progress of our nation and tarnish its fair fame. They should therefore receive the indignant frowns of every good citizen who sincerely loved his country and takes a pride in its prosperity and honor.

Our Constitution, though not perfect, is doubtless the best that ever was formed. Therefore let every proposition to change it be well weighed and, if found beneficial, cautiously adopted. Every patriot will rejoice to see its authority so exerted as to advance the prosperity and honor of the nation, whilst he will watch with jealousy any attempt to mutilate this charter of our liberties or pervert its powers to acts of aggression or injustice. Thus shall conservatism and progress blend their harmonious action in preserving the form and spirit of the Constitution and at the same time carry forward the great improvements of the country with a rapidity and energy which freemen only can display.

In closing this my last annual communication, permit me, fellow-citizens, to congratulate you on the prosperous condition of our beloved country. Abroad its relations with all foreign powers are friendly, its rights are respected, and its high place in the family of nations cheerfully recognized. At home we enjoy an amount of happiness, public and private, which has probably never fallen to the lot of any other people. Besides affording to our own citizens a degree of prosperity of which on so large a scale I know of no other instance, our country is annually affording a refuge and a home to multitudes, altogether without example, from the Old World.

BIBLIOGRAPHICAL AIDS

BIBLIOGRAPHICAL AIDS

The emphasis in this and subsequent volumes in the Presidential Chronologies series will be on the administrations of the presidents. The more important works on other aspects of their lives, either before or after their terms, are included since they may contribute to an understanding of the presidential careers.

The following bibliography is critically selected. An extensive bibliography on Taylor's life may be found in the Hamilton biography, and that of Fillmore in the Rayback biography. (See biographies below) and in the standard guides. The student might also wish to consult Reader's Guide to Periodical Literature and Social Sciences and Humanities Index (formerly International Index) for recent articles in scholarly journals.

Additional chronolgical information not included in this volume because it did not relate directly to the president may be found in the Encyclopedia of American History, edited by Richard B. Morris, revised edition (New York, 1965).

Asterisks after titles refer to books currently available in paperback editions.

ZACHARY TAYLOR
SOURCE MATERIALS

Zachary Taylor made frequent notations about his army life, his early political feelings, and his journey to the White House. They are collected and held in the Manuscript Division of the Library of Congress, Washington, D.C. under the title Autobiographical Sketch. Also at the Library of Congress are the Zachary Taylor Ppaers, with many of his personal remarks about the 1849-1850 crisis.

Buchanan, James. Manuscript. Historical Society of Pennsylvania, Philadelphia. Casts light on the controversy of 1850, and illuminates the character and role of Zachary Taylor.

Quaife, Milo M., ed. The Diary of James K. Polk During his Presidency. Four volumes, Chicago, 1910. Polk's comments about

Taylor's role in the Mexican War, and the hero's subsequent political rise makes entertaining and enlightening reading.

Weed, Thurlow, Papers. Rochester. The very active part played by the New York Whig "boss" in the selection, the election, and the short presidential term of Taylor, provides an excursion into how presidents were made around 1850.

Dyer, Brainerd. Zachary Taylor. Baton Rouge, 1946. Excellent details involving the major events of Taylor's executive-legislative struggle. A liberal use of manuscripts and letters add to the scholarship.

Hamilton, Holman. Zachary Taylor. Two volumes. New York, (1941, 1953). The best and fullest treatment of Taylor for the general reader. The first volume includes Taylor's life as an army man and national hero, and is a fine source of information on the early Indian wars, and, of course, the war with Mexico. Taylor's behavior as President is also better understood when viewed within the perspective of Taylor's lifelong experiences. Volume two considers the aged President's trials in the White House, and his relations with some of the most independent-minded politicians in American history. Both volumes are quite readable, with some stretches of tedium.

Howard, Oliver Otis. General Taylor. New York, 1892. An early biography, generally informative, but the man never seems to be quite believeable.

McKinley, Silas B. and Silas Bent. Old Rough and Ready. New York, 1946. Not as informative as one would expect; the authors elected William Brown as Speaker of the House rather than Howell Cobb, in the emotional House election of 1849 — not an unimportant oversight.

ESSAYS

Very general treatments of the life and times of President Taylor are contained in the Encyclopedia Britannica, and the Americana Encyclopedia. The research student should not rely on either of these for any substantial information. The treatment of Taylor in the Dictionary of American Biography by Wendell H. Stephenson, is more detailed, but still too superficial.

Foster, Herbert D. "Webster's Seventh of March Speech and the Secession Movement, 1850", American Historical Review. Jan., 1922, pp. 245-270. Stresses the reactions of the sourthern political leaders to the image of Union.

Hamilton, Holman. "Democratic Senate Leadership and the Compromise of 1850", Mississippi Valley Historical Review, Dec., 1954, pp. 403-418. Explores the evolution of Senate thinking from regional sectionalism to the realization of an actual split in the nation, and thus to compromise.

Hodder, Frank H. "The Authorship of the Compromise of 1850", Mississippi Valley Historical Review, March, 1936, pp. 525-536. Details the rarely mentioned but extremely important part played by Senator Stephen A. Douglas of Illinois in directing the Senate's thinking towards final agreement in the crisis of 1850.

Lavender, David. "How to Make it to the White House Without Really Trying", American Heritage, June, 1967, 26ff. An amusing account of how General Taylor used James K. Polk to feather his own political nest.

Sellers, Charles G. "Who Were the Southern Whigs?", Historical Vistas, ed. Grady McWhiney, Robert Wiebe, Boston, 1963,* pp. 366-379. Develops the framework for the growth of the Whig Party in the South, and analyzes the reasons for its success.

MONOGRAPHS AND SPECIAL AREAS

Going, Charles B. David Wilmot, Free-Soiler; a Biography of the Great Advocate of the Wilmot Proviso. New York, 1924. The story of the man who started one of the most momentous debates in American history.

Jameson, J. Franklin, ed. Correspondence of John C. Calhoun. American Historical Association, Annual Report, 1899, Washington, 1900. President Taylor's strained relationship with Senator

Calhoun is better appreciated after a perusal of some of the "great nullifier's" letters.

Merk, Frederick. Manifest Destiny and Mission in American History: a reinterpretation. New York, 1963. The author present the events and personalities leading to the Compromise of 1850, and the Whig's stand against the war with Mexico.

Smith, Elber B. Magnificent Missourian: the Life of Thomas Hart Benton. Philadelphia, 1958. Benton's position in the United States Senate commanded the attention of the entire nation, especially when he aired his views on the nature of slavery extension.

MILLARD FILLMORE
SOURCE MATERIALS

Almost all of the available papers of Millard Fillmore are held by the Buffalo Historical Society. Three volumes, edited by F.H. Severance, and entitled Millard Fillmore Papers, form the basis of the collection. On March 29, 1969, the New York Times announced the discovery of over 10,000 items relating to Fillmore, including 70 or 80 letters from Dorothea Dix; the collection was found in a New Haven, New York farmhouse. The State University of New York at Oswego has control over these materials. This rather startling discovery will, hopefully, add significantly to the rather sparse materials now on hand.

Seward, William H. Papers. Rochester. The turbulant relationship between Fillmore and the New York senator was an important factor in the political independence epitomized by the President.

Weed, Thurlow. Life of Thurlow Weed including his Autobiography and a Memoir. Two volumes, Boston, 1883-1884. Unfortunately the most widely quoted source on the character of Millard Fillmore. Weed's opinion of the "incorruptible man from Buffalo" created part of the myth that Fillmore was a man of limited talents, and probably a bigot.

BIOGRAPHIES

Griffis, William E. Millard Fillmore. Ithaca, 1915. The earlier biography that has been eclipsed by Rayback's fuller study.

Rayback, Robert J. Millard Fillmore, Biography of a President. Buffalo, 1959. The most inclusive biography to date, and the volume
that finally dispels the image of Fillmore as an "anti-Catholic
bigot." The reader is impressed not only with the scholarship
in evidence on every page, but that the entire book is consis-
tently readable. An added filip is the exciting story of western
New York State, as it grew from the sleepy, rural frontier into
a politically important industrial region, a region that gave
birth to some of the most important political traditions in
American history.

ESSAYS

Overly brief descriptions of the Fillmore administration are contained in the Encyclopedia Britannica, and the Americana Encyclopedia. Neither of these should be used as the only sources for an ade-
quate coverage of Fillmore's years. Julius W. Pratt's treatment of
Fillmore in the Dictionary of American Biography is very good, but
has a few gaps in information.

Degler, Carl N. "There was Another South," American Heritage,
August, 1960, 53 ff. Pinpoints some famous southern unionists
of the 1850's, many of whom were ardent supporters of President Fillmore.

Russel, Robert R. "What was the Compromise of 1850?," Journal of
Southern History, August, 1956, pp. 292-309. Illustrates the
behind-the-scenes conferences that led to the famous compromise.

St. George, L. Sioussat. "Tennessee, the Compromise of 1850, and
the Nashville Convention", Mississippi Valley Historical Review, Dec, 1915, pp. 313-347. The elements of political dis-
trust, economic problems, and a threatened civilization are examined as important stepping-stones to southern unification.

Van Alstyne, R.W. "British Diplomacy and the Clayton-Bulwer Treaty,
1850-1856", Journal of Modern History Volume 9, 1939, pp.
157-164. An account of the numerous semantic misunderstand-
ings that plagued the Taylor-Fillmore administrations.

MONOGRAPHS AND SPECIAL AREAS

Hale, Edward Everett. William H. Seward. Philadelphia, 1910. An excellent, if flattering, biography of the famous man who was

once a political thorn in Fillmore's side.

Hamilton, Holman. Prologue to Conflict: the Crisis and Compromise of 1850. Lexington, 1964. A very useful volume, especially the excellent appendices of the congressional roll calls on the various bills that eventually became the Compromise of 1850.

Phillips, Ulrich B., ed. Correspondence of Robert Toombs, Alexander H. Stephens, and Howell Cobb. Annual Report, American Historical Association. Washington, D.C., 1913. Three men of the South, and the fascinating roles each played in setting the American republic on a different course.

————. The Southern Whigs, 1834-1954. New York, 1910. Traces the Whig Party from its conception to its ultimate collapse. It is interesting to consider this volume along with the accounts of Whig growth in the North.

Russel, Robert R. "The General Effects of Slavery upon Southern Economic Progress", Journal of Southern History, February, 1938, pp. 34-54. The author refutes some of the generalizations on the topic, and convinces the reader that he has some good ammunition.

THE TAYLOR – FILLMORE YEARS

Andrist, Ralph K., ed. The American Heritage History of the Making of the Nation. New York, 1968, pp. 337-398. A nicely illustrated and well written account of the most significant events of the 1850's.

Billington, Ray A. The Protestant Crusade, 1800-1860. New York, 1938. Tells all the tales that have been deleted from the secondary school texts. The role of Millard Fillmore as the Know-Nothing candidate for the presidency is treated in an objective manner.

Craven, Avery O. The Growth of Southern Nationalism, 1848-1861. Baton Rouge, 1953. Already a classic in its field.

Filler, Louis. The Crusade Against Slavery, 1830-1860. New York, 1960. Lively characterizations of the Abolitionists and their supporters.

Floan, Howard P. The South in Northern Eyes, 1831-1861. Austin, 1958. A fascinating study of how the North developed and enlarged its stereotyped image of the South.

Gara, Larry. The Liberty Line: The Legend of the Underground Railroad. Lexington, 1961.

Nevins, Allan. Ordeal of the Union: Fruits of Manifest Destiny. Volume 1, New York, 1947. Nevins forcuses on the political forces
of these difficult years, and tells the gripping story with style
and color.

Russell, Robert R. Economic Aspects of Southern Sectionalism, 1840-
1861. New York, 1924. How passions heated as the cotton
prices rose and fell, and its effects on the American republic.

Smith, T.C. Parties and Slavery, 1850-1859. New York, 1906. An old
volume, but surprisingly readable and instructive.

Van Deusen, Glyndon G. The Life of Henry Clay. Boston, 1937. This
biography has been considered the definitive work on its subject.

Wiltse, Charles M. John C. Calhoun: Sectionalist, 1840-1850. The
author searches deeply into the motivations of the famous mul-
lifer, and succeeds in developing a sense of awe and respect.

THE PRESIDENCY

American Heritage Publication. History of the President of the United
States. New York, 1968. A lavishly illustrated and informative
discussion of the men in the White House.

Bailey, Thomas A. Presidential Greatness: The Image and the Man
from George Washington to the Present. New York, 1966.*
An entertaining and instructive volume. The author ranks
Zachary Taylor in the "below average" group of United
States Presidents, and Millard Fillmore is ranked as "aver-
age."

Corwin, Edward S. The President: Office and Powers. Fourth edition,
New York, 1957.

Kane, Joseph N. Facts About the Presidents. New York, 1959. A
useful listing of data about each President, his cabinet, his
personal life, and his achievements.

Laski, Harold J. The American Presidency. New York, 1940.

Schlesinger, Arthur M. "Historians Rate United States Presidents",
Life, Nov. 1, 1948, p. 65. Taylor is ranked twenty-fifth in the

the quality rating list, and falls into the "below average" category; Fillmore ranks just above, in the twenty-fourth position, but still "below average."

————. "Our Presidents: A Rating by Seventy-five Historians". New York Times Magazine, July 29, 1962, 12ff. Both Fillmore and Taylor rise within the ranks of the "below average" category, but with Taylor superseding Fillmore.

NAME INDEX

Adams, Charles F., 13, 14, 15
Adams, John Q., 50
Alligator, Chief, 6
Allison, John S., 12
Ampudia, Pedro de, 9
Arista, Mariano, 9
Armistad, Walker, K., 6
Atchinson, David R., 16

Babcock, George, 62
Bancroft, George, 7
Benton, Thomas H., 18, 21
Biddle, Nicholas, 53
Bliss, William S., 7, 15, 24
Branch, Judge, 58
Buchanan, James, 66
Buell, Don Carlos, 7
Bullitt, Alexander C., 15
Burr, Aaron, 2
Butler, William O., 12

Calhoun, John C., 16, 21
Cass, Lewis, 12, 15
Clay, Henry, 12, 13, 18, 19, 20,
   21, 22, 24, 50, 56, 61
Clayton, John M., 12, 17, 19, 21
Clingham, Thomas L., 18
Cobb, Howell, 18
Collamer, Jacob, 17
Collier, John A., 57
Crawford, George W., 17
Crittenden, John J., 12 .

Dallas, George M., 17
Davis, Jefferson, 5, 7
Dodge, Henry, 17
Donelson, Andrew 65
Douglas, Stephen A., 20, 64

Ellmacer, Amos, 51
Ewing, Thomas, 14, 17

Fillmore, Abigail Powers (wife), 49,
   50, 63, 64
Fillmore, Caroline C. McIntosh (2nd
   wife), 66
Fillmore, Mary Abigail (daughter),
   51, 65
Fillmore, Millard Powers (son), 50
Fillmore, Nathaniel (father), 49
Fillmore, Phoebe Millard (mother), 49
Fish, Hamilton, 58, 60
Flagg, Azariah C., 57
Foote, Charles, 14
Foote, Henry, 21
Frelinghuysen, Theodore, 56
Fremont, John C., 66

Gidding, Joshua, 14
Graham, William S., 62
Grant, Ulysses S., 7
Greeley, Horace, 56, 65

Hale, John P., 62
Hall, Nathan K., 50, 51
Harrison, William Henry, 1, 54, 55
Haven, Solomon G., 51
Hawk, Black, 5
Hopkins, Samuel, 2
Hunt, Washington, 60

Ingersoll, Joseph, 10

Jackson, Andrew, 2, 6, 52
Jesup, Thomas, 6
Johnson, Andrew, 67
Johnson, Reverdy, 17

117

118